# EAST AFRICA

# EAST AFRICA

## BY LAWRENCE FELLOWS

The Macmillan Company, New York, New York
Collier-Macmillan Ltd., London

For Eva and Robin

The Macmillan Company
866 Third Avenue, New York, N.Y. 10022
Collier-Macmillan Canada Ltd., Toronto, Ontario
Library of Congress catalog card number: 76-165108
*Map by Rafael Palacios*
Printed in the United States of America

10  9  8  7  6  5  4  3  2  1

Acknowledgment is due to the following publishers for kindly giving permission to
quote from copyright material:
   *East Africa Journal*, Nairobi, Kenya, for passages from H. W. O. Okoth Ogendo's
poem, "The Flames of Consciousness," and Lennard Okola's poem, "A Voice in the
Dark."
   *Nanga*, the English Department magazine of National Teachers' College Kyam-
bogo, Kampala, Uganda, for a passage from Okumu pa'Lukobo's poem, "The
Poacher's Lament."
   Présence Africaine, Paris, France, for extracts from Aimé Césaire's *Cahier d'un
Retour au Pays Natal* (*Return to My Native Land*), translated by Émile Snyder
and with a preface by André Breton, published by Présence Africaine, Paris
(1971).

*Title page photo: A Masai boy and his cattle herd; in the background,
Mt. Meru in northern Tanzania*

# CONTENTS

# CHAPTER 1

# THE EAST AFRICAN SETTING

East Africa is a land of endless variety, a land of quick and vivid contrasts. It has fertile slopes and valleys and harsh, forbidding plains where nothing grows but thorn trees and bush. It has turbulent waterfalls and immense, mauve-green stretches of uninhabited swamp. Its snow-topped mountains are the highest on the African continent, its lakes the deepest. It has desert landscapes so tortured by the relentless sun and so barren that neither man nor beast can survive, and forests so dense that not even the sun can penetrate them.

There is a profusion of wildlife: elephants, rhinos, buffaloes, giraffes, lions, leopards, water birds and giant forest birds, horny-scaled reptiles, militant columns of safari ants. They are all parts of the spectacular, intricately balanced landscape.

There are primitive villages, modern cities and remnants of exotic old kingdoms. There is a bewildering array of people and customs. These are the three countries usually referred to as East Africa: Kenya, Uganda and Tanzania. They have been set together by a shared history of wars, famines, migrations, by

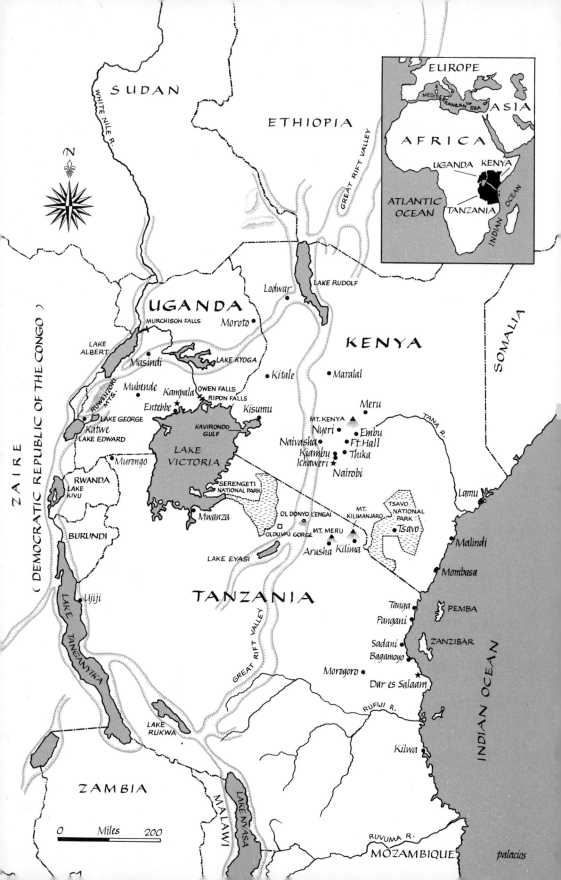

the trading in slaves and ivory and by the trials of colonization and independence. They have been set apart from the rest of the African continent by the Great Rift Valley, a double line of deep, irregular, troughlike depressions that were torn into the surface of the earth when it shifted and heaved in some anguished, prehistoric geological age.

The Rift Valley's four-thousand-mile course of upheaval begins far north of the African continent, in southern Turkey. It follows a line of twisted hills and ruptured earth and water-filled declivities through the Sea of Galilee and the Dead Sea and cuts into Africa at the southern end of the Red Sea. It enters Kenya from Ethiopia's rugged southern hills at Lake Rudolf— the "Jade Sea," set in a hot, wind-blown world of sand and sun-scorched rock.

Down the eastern side of Lake Victoria, the eastern course of the Rift Valley dissipates in a line of crusted, crystalline lakes, of rounded hills and eroded valleys filled with the rubble of ancient lava flows. Of the volcanoes that rise from the floor of the valley, Ol Donyo L'Engai, in Tanzania, still rumbles with activity every six years. It erupts violently every twelve years, as it did in 1966, with a deafening noise and an awesome display of fury and lightning flashes. A pillar of hot volcanic ash is thrown ten thousand feet into the air, to nearly twice the height of the volcano, and spread for twenty miles around. Ol Donyo L'Engai in the Masai language means "Mountain of God."

West of Lake Victoria, the Rift Valley branches off into a parallel course and follows another great crescent of lakes and mountains several hundred miles away. Then it veers eastward to join the other line of the Rift Valley through Malawi and Mozambique to the sea.

With an area of 26,828 square miles, Lake Victoria is the largest in Africa; it is almost the size of Scotland. At the start of the western course of the Rift Valley is Lake Tanganyika, about four hundred miles long, more than half as long as California, and occasionally tempestuous. It is 4,706 feet deep, deeper than any other on the continent.

On the edge of the valley's western course rise the towering, mist-hidden peaks of the Ruwenzori Mountains, the fabled "Mountains of the Moon" which Ptolemy, the Alexandrian geographer, marked on his map in the second century A.D. as *Lunae Montes Finis Orientalis*. Ptolemy suggested that these mountains were the source of the Nile, a tantalizing prospect that caused romantics and explorers to seek the Nile's source and the mountains, and to venture guesses about them for the next seventeen centuries.

The Ruwenzori Mountains in Uganda are a towering presence of mighty spurs and forest-clad crevasses that roll away from sight behind a misty curtain. It is a fantastic world of bog and moss, a spongy mass of rotting vegetation, heaths draped in lichen, clouds of brilliant butterflies, mahogany trees 170 feet tall festooned with ferns and tender orchids. At times the mist lifts briefly, but then dense clouds rush up the valleys, blotting out everything again.

These, roughly, are the barriers that contain East Africa, a vast area of 680,000 square miles. In 1970 more than thirty-three million people lived there: eleven million in Kenya, eight and a half million in Uganda, more than thirteen million in Tanzania. They are as varied as the landscape, rooted in hundreds of different traditions, different languages, different origins.

Yet many of the problems they face are the same: they became independent in quick succession. At first there were four countries. Tanganyika got its independence on December 9, 1961; Uganda on October 9, 1962; Zanzibar on December 10, 1963; and Kenya on December 12, 1963. Zanzibar had been independent only a month when the island was swept by a violent revolution that drove the Sultan from power. On April 22, 1964, Tanganyika and Zanzibar formed a union, and called it Tanzania.

The idea of nationhood is still largely an abstraction to most of these people. The whole concept of nationhood was not theirs in the first place. It was introduced by British and German colonialists who were marking out areas of influence and exclusive trade for themselves. The Arabs and Portuguese before them were essentially seafaring people, content to man their fortress islands and the ports through which their trade in ivory and slaves flowed. Before the Arabs and Portuguese arrived in East Africa, it was a precarious and shifting battleground for hundreds of peaceful or marauding tribes and tiny, independent kingdoms, respecting rough frontiers or none at all. For the most part, their stories are buried in the undiscovered or lost chapters of human history.

There are scraps of evidence that East Africa may even have been the cradle of humanity. At Olduvai Gorge in Tanzania, at Kanam on the shore of Lake Victoria in Kavirondo Gulf, on Rusinga Island in the lake and at Fort Ternan and Lothagam Hill in Kenya, the oldest evidence of man and his manlike ancestors has been unearthed, some of it twenty million years old. These bits of jawbone and skull have been studied more systematically than have the cultures that later helped to shape East Africa. But the later waves of people had no written languages and no calendar and left no visual record apart from some iron workings and some scattered rock paintings of human figures and animals in a dozen different styles. Very little about them can be discerned now from African music and poetry, or distilled now from the traditional histories and mythologies that have been told and retold by generations of tribal elders. Little remains of the past, because little was permanent. Among the tribes that were concerned with the order of things, there was always an inclination to accept the natural, and to find simple explanations for their origins and the things around them that they did not understand.

Among the Nilotic tribes, who are presumed to have begun moving southward up the Nile Valley toward the end of the fifteenth century, and who have established themselves in the centuries since around Lake Victoria and across the northern half of Uganda, there is a recurring story of a supreme being who created man from clay. The Lango, a Nilotic tribe in Uganda, related that Olum, the first Lango, was fashioned from clay in the sky by Jok, and then sent to earth to father the human race. The Acholi, another Nilotic tribe that is spread northward from

Lango territory to the southern Sudan, tell the same story, but about themselves. They add that Jok also fashioned animals and plants in the sky, and sent them to earth.

The Bantu tribes are a race apart from the Nilotes, and came from other directions. Most of the Bantu tribes were already wandering into East Africa in the fifteenth century before the Nilotes began to come. Hunters and fishermen and shifting cultivators, they spread from the center of Africa across the southern half of Uganda into Kenya. In much later stages, they moved northward up the coastal plain through Tanzania and deep into Kenya. They, too, believed very often in a supreme being, although he sat usually atop a snow-capped mountain or somewhere else out of reach. He was approached and appeased through ancestor-spirits residing in hills more easily climbed or, as with the Kikuyu and some other Bantu tribes in Kenya, through ancestor-spirits residing in sacred trees. For the Kikuyu, Ngai was the Divider of the Universe and he lived on the jagged peaks of Mount Kenya, 17,058 feet high. An attempt to climb those glaciers to get close to Ngai could cause a man to freeze to death, even though Mount Kenya lies astride the equator.

Kilimanjaro is just as sacred to the tribes around its base, and one of its two peaks, Kibo, at 19,340 feet, is the highest in Africa. The name comes from the Chagga words *Kilima,* for "mountain," and *Njaro,* which means "glittering." Most of the tribes within sight of it have their own names for Kilimanjaro, and many legends about it, including one that dates from the time when Kibo was still a smoldering volcano and Mawenzi, the lesser peak, was already dormant. Kibo, according to the story, was pestered by his older brother, Mawenzi, for a light for his pipe, because it had stopped smoking. Kibo finally lost his patience and clubbed Mawenzi viciously, leaving him several notches shorter, at 16,896 feet, and with a rather flattened and battered-looking peak. Eventually Kibo's pipe stopped smoking, too.

In the saddle between Kibo and Mawenzi are two red hills called the Fire Mountains. Tribes took sacrifices to the ancestor-

*Mt. Kilimanjaro, seen from the town of Moshi in Tanzania*

spirits they thought resided there, the weird rushing sound of voices being heard in the wind in the hills and in the caves around them.

Among the Masai, one of the cattleherding Nilo-Hamitic peoples, a race apart from both the Nilotes and the Bantu, there are legends of an ancestor called Maasinda who made a great ladder to help the Masai climb from Lake Rudolf onto the Uasin Gishu plateau north of Kitale, in Kenya. The Masai spread over the central part of the Kenya highlands, possibly at the end of the sixteenth century, and southward down the Rift Valley into Tanzania.

Although the Masai and other Nilo-Hamites who followed them into East Africa became very mixed racially with Bantu and Nilotic tribes, they are believed to have originated from much farther away than Lake Rudolf. They are lean and lighter in color than most of the Bantu and Nilotes, and have a narrower build and finer bone structure. The Hamites originated in the river civilizations of the Euphrates and Tigris, and this stream of the race is presumed to have spread to Egypt and up the Nile, hence the name Nilo-Hamites.

On the coastal plain another stream of Hamites moved much later into East Africa, presumably having wandered down the Arabian peninsula over the centuries, across to the Horn of Africa, then down through the northern desert in search of water and grazing for their herds of camels and cattle.

The Galla and the Somali and other Hamitic tribes pushing southward down the coast blocked the northward migration of Bantu tribes. The Arabs who sailed by dhow from the Arabian peninsula and settled on the coast were Hamites, too.

When the Masai and other Nilo-Hamites pressed southward over the grazing land they wanted for their cattle, they forced the Kamba, Taita, Meru, Kikuyu and other Bantu tribes onto the steep slopes and into the thick forests at the edges of the Rift Valley, where they were relatively undisturbed and turned increasingly to agriculture, and where their folklore was colored by the trees and hills and things that were a part of their new homelands.

The Baganda, a big and prosperous and accomplished Bantu people in Uganda, have a whole array of heavenly beings to direct and explain their lives for them, beginning with Kintu and his wife, Nambi, who came to earth from Gulu, which is their word for heaven, to father the Baganda people. The heavenly figures of the Baganda are sometimes inclined to mischief, as was Walumbe, one of Nambi's brothers, who tried once to intercept her on a trip back to Gulu to get food for her hen. Another brother, Kaikusi, heard of Walumbe's plan, and chased him into one of the holes in the ground at Tanda. Whenever Walumbe stuck his head above ground, Kaikusi would swing his club at him, only to see his brother disappear into the hole just in time, and then reappear briefly from another hole. The story does not reveal much about the mysterious holes in the ground at Tanda, but it helps to illustrate the elusive nature of tribal mythology, and of East Africa's past.

There are tribes that do not fit easily into any of the bigger groupings. In the Mau Forest of Kenya there are the Ndorobo, a hapless remnant of the earliest inhabitants of Kenya who still try to live only by hunting. In the Ituri Rain Forest, on the far side of the Ruwenzori Mountains, there are pygmies who live by the snakes they catch and the monkeys they net or bring down with their tiny bows and poisoned arrows. Close to the pygmies, on the slopes of the mountains, are the Bwamba and Bakonjo tribes, only slightly larger than the pygmies, and living much of the time in rebellion against the Uganda government. Every few months the rebellion springs to life and these wizened, wrinkled little men, their bodies painted white with mud and their teeth filed to points, come screaming down from the slopes to throw a few spears at a market or a police station, and then run screaming into the dense forest again. On the treeless, sun-baked shore of Lake Rudolf, the last hundred families of the El Molo tribe survive. The Galla gave them their name, which means "poor devils," but no one is sure of the tribe's origin. The El Molo insist they are descended from a fish, and are content to stay where they are, surviving on lake fish and the highly alkaline water.

Somali herdsmen prepare
to bring their cattle
across the Tana River
in Kenya during a
500-mile cattle drive
from Somalia to the
slaughterhouses in
Mombasa

There are 68 tribes of significant size in Kenya, 36 in Uganda and 128 in Tanzania. Each has its own set of traditions, its own form of tribal government, its own language, its own way of life. Some tribes are pastoral, some are cultivators, some fishermen. Even now, some are constantly at war with others, and their differences seem irreconcilable. The Bantu are as different from the Nilotes or the Hamites or the Nilo-Hamites as are the Chinese from the Indians.

But life is changing rapidly for the tribesmen and they drift increasingly into the cities, attracted by the broad avenues and bright lights and the babel of languages, by the frail hope of paid employment or the fair assurance of excitement. They flock especially to the capital cities: Nairobi in Kenya; Kampala in Uganda; Dar es Salaam in Tanzania.

In East Africa there are also British, Greeks, Germans, Dutch and Italians in large numbers, some working as civil servants, some representing commercial or industrial firms in their own countries, some living still on their old farms in the highlands or on the coastal plain, some from the big tea or coffee estates or sisal plantations. There are missionary priests, their soutanes often stained by red murram dust from their long road trips in from the mission stations in the bush. There are Arabs and Indians and Africans who have begun to covet white-collar respectability and European dress and manners.

Flowers grace all the bigger cities: hibiscus, jacaranda, frangipani, yellow-flowering acacias, bougainvillea. Something is always in blossom, in rich mauves and oranges and reds. The colors are mimicked in the dresses of the African women who pad along the roadsides with baskets brimming with goods for market. The mass of Africans in the towns belong somewhere in the half-light between the darkness that remains of East Africa's past and the glare of a strange, modern world. They are losing the security of their old tribal societies, and are just enough a part of the new economic system to be baffled by it.

Nairobi, with half a million people, was not so long ago an empty plain alongside a swamp at the foot of the Kikuyu hills. The plain was the exclusive preserve of the Masai then, and they knew it as *Uaso N'airobi*, "the place of the cold water." Toward the end of the nineteenth century, when the British were building a railroad into the interior, a party of Royal Engineers stopped on the plain and built a depot for their rails and ties and other equipment. They put up a thorn fence to protect their mules from marauding lions and from the angry Masai, and from this encampment the city grew.

Kampala was *Kasozi ka M'pala*, which means the "hill of the impala" in the elusive language of the Baganda, as the people of the tribe are called. As with most Bantu languages, the prefix changes the meaning of the word: thus, a member of the tribe is Muganda; the name of the tribal kingdom was Buganda; the language is Luganda; the adjective for most things pertaining to the tribe is Kiganda.

*Aerial view of Nairobi, the capital of Kenya*

The Swahili-speaking interpreters for the first English explorers to reach Kampala were baffled, and called the place Uganda for simplicity's sake; the name stuck to the larger country.

The words *Kasozi ka M'pala* were not spoken completely. *Kasozi,* the word for hill, was understood but rarely uttered; the Baganda called the hill merely *ka M'pala,* meaning "of the impala." That name stuck, too, and spreads now over twenty hills, over a town where high, modern buildings rise from among the deep green canopies of coffee trees and the drooping fronds of banana and plantain.

But, as in Rome and Lisbon, only seven hills are counted, the most important of which was not Kampala, but Mengo, which means "millstones." Mengo was the traditional seat of the king, the Kabaka of Buganda, from the time Mutesa I established residence there in 1895, and built a palace overlooking the hill opposite, with the impala grazing peacefully there.

In Mutesa's time Buganda was one of the most highly developed governments in tropical Africa. It had a parliament, a prime minister, courts of law, a huge bureaucracy and a royal family that traced its lineage back for four centuries. Buganda was the biggest and richest of the forty or more powerful, rival kingdoms that were spread in the nineteenth century across Uganda and down into the oval of lakes from Lake Kyoga in the north to Lake Tanganyika in the south. With the approach of independence from Britain the Kabaka of Buganda wanted nothing to do with a united Uganda, unless he could control it. He intrigued for a separate independence for Buganda until the kingdoms in Uganda were finally suppressed after Uganda got its independence as a single state.

Dar es Salaam was a small fishing village until Sultan Majid of Zanzibar built a residence there in 1862, and gave it its name. In Arabic it means "haven of peace." The Germans, in the days when Tanganyika was their colony, made Dar es Salaam the capital because of its splendid harbor. The city has witnessed a great deal of bewildering, sometimes chaotic, political change since then, but certain things remain the same: the easy manner and open smiles and poverty of the people, the oppressive heat and the mosquito nets, the paddling of overhead fans, the sticky nights at crowded bars where sailors and airline pilots and the expatriates of many countries talk about the mysteries of the place, the strange and often startling things that have happened to them in East Africa and the secrets the land still retains.

There is an old saying in Swahili that a person once bitten by a snake will be startled even by a palm. On the coast of East Africa there are many palms. Their slender, branchless boles rise all around, swaying in the baffling winds, yet reaching always toward the sea. It was to the sea that this remote land, so long a mystery to the outside world, first began to release its secrets.

# CHAPTER 2

# THE PAST

From December to March, during daylight hours, the northeast monsoon blows strongly off the Indian Ocean, bringing with it the dhows of Arabia. For centuries Arabs have sailed in fleets of these ancient-looking wooden ships with their high poops and huge, triangular sails, and carried their trade far down the East African coast to the humid, coral-girt harbors of Mombasa and Dar es Salaam and beyond.

The dhows are laden with handwoven carpets, intricately worked trinkets of silver and brass, bolts of printed and em- broidered cloth, brass-studded wooden chests, glass and beads, dates and even chunks of the dried shark meat that is savored by Arabs who live on the East coast of Africa. These are the descendants of the first Arabs who arrived from Muscat and Oman, or from Shiraz, and stayed.

The dhow captains cannot sail back until the monsoon turns and blows the other way. Until it does, the lean and turbaned sailors lounge about in the narrow streets, in the shade of flaking, whitewashed buildings. The idle sailors sip coffee and talk, and from time to time supervise the repair of their vessels. The Arab sailors wait through the warm weeks of spring for clouds to build up over the Mozambique Channel. This is the sign that the monsoon is shifting, that it will soon be blowing the other way.

Then, from May to October, when the monsoon blows from the southeast, the dhows sail away again with cargoes from East Africa: charcoal, grain, copra, mangrove poles to reinforce the mud houses in Arabia, ivory for Arabian and Indian carvers.

In 1970 a hundred dhows were still calling each season at the ports in East Africa, but this was a small show against the heavy sea traffic of earlier, more lucrative days. Before the Portuguese arrived to compete for control of the coast, and before the slave trade was finally abolished, as many as seven hundred Arab dhows called each season at Mombasa alone.

For centuries the Arabs had dominated trade not only with East Africa, but over the whole of the Indian Ocean, to Mesopotamia, Persia, the Indus Valley and beyond to the Far East. The Arabs braved the heat and the treacherous, funneling winds of the Red Sea to meet caravans that would carry their goods across the desert to the cities of Egypt.

Before the nineteenth century East Africa was known to the rest of the world only by its coast. Nothing of the history of the vast interior was written down. Almost nothing of the great upheavals going on in the interior was known to the outside world. The Bantu migrations from the Congo River basin were still in progress and the Bushmen and other older inhabitants of East Africa were fleeing ahead of these newcomers, heading into the thick forests or to the hot, inhospitable deserts where they felt no one would follow and harass them.

Not much of the Arab past on the coast was recorded either, but some of the past lingers. Much of it still lies hidden in the ruins of Gedi and Kilwa, and in the narrow streets of Mombasa's old town. The historians have been left only a few written texts to draw upon, beginning with parts of a document called the Periplus of the Erythraean Sea.

A periplus is an account of a voyage. Eritrea eventually became a coastal province of Ethiopia, but the Erythraean Sea was the

*Ruins of the once busy town of Gedi*

name used in the Graeco-Roman world for the whole expanse of
ocean from the coast of Africa to the farthest known corners of
the east.

The Alexandrian merchant who wrote this account of his
voyage into the Indian Ocean, and whose name is not known,
described his passage from Egypt to the ports of Arabia as far
as Kane, and to Azania, as the coast of East Africa was known
in his part of the world. The account may have been written as
early as the middle of the first century A.D. At his farthest port
of call on the Azanian coast, a trading post he referred to as
Rhapta, the Alexandrian was impressed by the extent of Arab
control on the coast even then. He wrote:

"It has an abundant supply of ivory and some turtle shell. The
inhabitants of this coast, men of huge stature, are given to
piracy; they live each in their own district, their own masters.
In accordance with some ancient right, this district is subject
to the sovereignty of the state that becomes most powerful in
Arabia, and so is now ruled by the Mapharitic chieftain. From

the king it is held tributary by the people of Muza who send there many ships with Arab captains and agents who enjoy the friendship of the natives, intermarry with them and thus become familiar with the coast and their language."

From this intermarriage of Arabs and Africans the Swahili people evolved. They are dark-skinned, and speak the Swahili language, a hybrid tongue that is basically a Bantu language, but heavily infused with foreign words. These were Arabic words at first, but words from Portuguese and English and even Urdu and Hindi from the Indian subcontinent have since enriched this language. Swahili became the trading language of the coast, and is still spreading into the interior. On Zanzibar, the people of mixed Arab and African ancestry were called Shirazi, the word originally used for the people, Arabs and Persians, who came from Shiraz, on the southern coast of Persia.

These venturesome people from Shiraz and Arabia came to the East African coast not in one great invasion, but in successive waves, especially in the centuries after the death of the Prophet Mohammed in 632 A.D. They spread the Moslem faith to East Africa, as they did to other tribes of Arabia, to Syria, Mesopotamia, Persia, India and across North Africa to Spain.

Not all those who ventured out to these places went only to spread word of the Moslem faith. There were disputes in the Arab world as to who was the rightful Caliph, or successor to the Prophet. Some of those on the losing side took refuge on the pleasant coast of East Africa. They called it Zenjibar or Zanjibar, meaning the "coast of the blacks," as the whole of the coast of East Africa was known then to the Arabs and Persians. The word *zenj* or *zanj* meant "black" and *bar* was the word for "coast."

Now the name Zanzibar applies only to the big coral island off the coast. It rose at one time to considerable economic and political power, for it was well-placed for entry to the mainland, and for putting to sail in the monsoon. The American clipper ships paid regular visits there in the days before steam, and had such a grip on the calico trade in Zanzibar that unprinted cotton cloth is still called Amerikani around the eastern part of the

African continent. The slave trade also flourished in Zanzibar. From there the Omani ruler, Seyyid Said bin Sultan, made his influence effective on the coast of East Africa from Cape Delgado to Lamu, and finally settled permanently on Zanzibar. The first European consulates in East Africa were established on Zanzibar.

It was once said that when Zanzibar played the flute all East Africa danced to it. But over the years, as better access to the continent was gained and the slave trade diminished, the island was deprived of its grim role as pied piper. Zanzibar became a backwater with the sweet smell of cloves in the air and the marks of recurring violence and despair on the faces of the people, part of the imperfect union that was forged with Tanganyika on April 22, 1964, as the United Republic of Tanzania.

*Twentieth century Arab sailors aboard a dhow*

Other places on the East African coast had their days of great power, including the island of Kilwa. It is a ruin now, a mere shadow of its former splendor. According to Arab legend, the first real settlement on the island was founded by Hasan bin Ali, a sultan of Shiraz, who had set sail from southern Persia with his family and followers in 975 A.D. in a fleet of dhows. The sultan and his six sons each founded a settlement. Hasan bin Ali must have regarded himself as a pioneer, but even he found someone had got to Kilwa ahead of him, according to an old Arab manuscript which reflects some of the suspicions and intrigues of the time:

"The newcomers found a Moslem already settled there with his family, and a mosque. From him they learned that the country belonged to the chief of the neighboring district of Amuli, who was then absent on a hunting expedition. After a few days he returned to Kilwa, and the stranger, being pleased with the island, offered, through the mediation of the friendly Moslem, to buy it. The chief named his terms, which were that the stranger should surround the whole island with colored cloth. This was soon done, and the chief took the cloth and surrendered the island. All the while, however, he cherished the secret intention of returning with an armed force to destroy the immigrants and carry off their goods. This was guessed by the Moslem, who had acted as an interpreter, so he warned the strangers to provide for their safety in time. Accordingly as soon as the chief's back was turned, they set to work and dug a trench in the neck of land joining Kilwa to the continent. After a short time the chief reappeared at the usual spot, and waited for the tide to go down and leave a dry passage to Kilwa; but the water never subsided, so he returned to his own country defeated and disappointed . . ."

Many of these early settlements were on islands, although some, like Mombasa, were separated from the mainland only by stretches of water almost as narrow as that at Kilwa. The Arabs fortified their islands and the towns grew up in the shelter of these defenses, looking rather like the towns in Arabia and Persia.

Indian traders, especially from Cambay, visited East Africa, too. Many of them settled there. From the East Indies the coconut palm, banana and tapioca plant were introduced to East Africa.

The Chinese had long had some hearsay knowledge of East Africa from Arabs carrying their trade up the coast of China. From China the Arabs took orange trees and silks and rhubarb, valued for its medicinal properties, to Africa. Chinese copper coins dating from 713 A.D. have been found at Kilwa.

A live giraffe was presented by Arab traders to the Emperor of China in 1414, a tribute to the strength and trading power of that vast nation. The Ming emperors of China sought to re-establish their prestige abroad, and sent several naval expeditions to the Indian Ocean. Two of these—one from 1417 to 1419, and another from 1421 to 1422—reached the coast of East Africa.

But the earliest trade and power on the coast belonged to the Arabs. In the three centuries before the Portuguese arrived— the thirteenth, fourteenth and fifteenth centuries—the Islamic civilization of the East African coast enjoyed its greatest days. To these centuries belong most of the splendid old palaces that remain on the coastline in more or less ruined state. On the island of Lamu, African huts of thatch and *boriti* poles are built against the remnants of walls that still show fine carvings in coral. The copper coinages of the sultans of Kilwa and Zanzibar still turn up on the beaches occasionally, as do the broken bits of Islamic and Chinese pottery. Fine Persian glazed bowls and Chinese porcelain had graced these Arab homes. Ming and celadon plates had been set on their tables or imbedded in the plaster walls for decoration.

When a Moroccan traveler, Ibn Battuta, visited the coast in 1331 he felt at home among the Moslems. He found Kilwa to be "a very fine and substantially built town" and, after spending a night in Mombasa, described the people there as "pious, honorable and upright." He marveled at the quantities of food these Arabs of East Africa consumed, at the regularity and abundance of meat dishes, and at the variety of fruit.

"One of these people eats as much as several of us," he wrote. "It is their custom."

Such was life for the Arabs in East Africa when Vasco da Gama rounded the Cape of Good Hope on his search for a new route to the fabled wealth of the East. He stopped at Mozambique Island long enough to indulge in a bit of plunder, and to take some prisoners. Word of this may have reached Mombasa ahead of him, for he got a wary reception there.

On Palm Sunday, 1498, the day after Vasco da Gama dropped anchor off Mombasa, the Sultan of Mombasa sent him some token gifts: a sheep, a few oranges and lemons, some sugar cane. The sultan also sent a ring as a pledge of safety and said that if the Portuguese would just bring their ships into the harbor, they would be given all the supplies they needed. To be doubly sure they were welcome, the Portuguese tried to pry some information about the Arabs' intentions from a couple of them they had captured. The questioning was severe, to judge from Vasco da Gama's own log:

"At night the captain-major questioned two Moors by dropping burning oil upon their skin, so that they might confess any treachery intended against us. They said that orders had been given to capture us as soon as we entered the port, and thus to avenge what we had done at Mozambique. And when this torture was being applied a second time, one of the Moors, although his hands were tied, threw himself into the sea, while the other did so during the morning watch."

The Arabs in Mombasa did make some attempts to sabotage the Portuguese, cutting the cable of one ship and the rigging of the mizzenmast of another. Vasco da Gama stayed until Thursday in spite of the trouble, and then left only to give chase to two small Arab vessels making for the open sea. He hoped to capture some booty, and possibly also a seaman who could pilot them onward to Calicut.

He did capture one of the vessels, with some gold and silver and seventeen people aboard, including a distinguished-looking old Moslem who told the Portuguese that four dhows from India stood anchored in Malindi, and that they would certainly have a navigator to spare, to guide the Portuguese on to the East.

The Portuguese anchored off Malindi on Easter Sunday, 1498,

*Dhows at the Old Port of Mombasa*

and set the captured Moslem down on a sandbank just in front of the town, with word of their arrival and of their friendly intentions.

On Monday the sultan returned the friendly greetings, along with gifts of food and spices. On Tuesday, approaching closer, the Portuguese received more gifts and an offer from the sultan to meet Vasco da Gama's captain in a boat. On Wednesday they met, not in the same boat, as the sultan had wanted, but in boats laying side by side. The two men exchanged pleasantries and talked about their future relations.

From a safe distance, Vasco da Gama made notes about the sultan's splendid display of pageantry, about his ornate garments and the attendants, most particularly the musicians with huge trumpets of ivory carved from elephant tusks.

The sultan supplied the Portuguese with an experienced sailor to guide them across the Indian Ocean to Calicut. It was the beginning of a long friendship between the Portuguese and the Arabs of Malindi, a matter of convenience for both. The Portuguese gained a foothold high up on the African coast, a strongpoint from which to protect their Indian Ocean trade and to supply their sailing ships on the long voyages to the East. The Sultan of Malindi had what he wanted: a powerful ally against his old enemy, the Sultan of Mombasa.

For the next decade the Portuguese tightened their grip on the East African coast; squadrons of Portuguese ships called at one harbor after another, demanding tribute to the Portuguese crown. With improved ships and firepower, the Portuguese were establishing themselves as the foremost naval power in the Indian Ocean. Sofala, Kilwa and Mombasa gave way, as did other places on the coast. Usually a small Portuguese garrison was left behind to ensure the loyalty of a place.

Mombasa remained troublesome, a thorn in the side of the Portuguese for the two centuries they ruled in East Africa. Several times the settlement was sacked and burned, but never in a scene so ludicrous and gruesome as that prompted in 1589 by the arrival of visitors from three sides.

A Turkish freebooter, Mirale Bey, came sailing down the coast looking for loot, as he had done three years before. On the first occasion he had told the people of Mombasa that he had been sent to rescue them, and did help them drive the Portuguese out of Mombasa. When the Portuguese viceroy at Goa heard the news from Malindi, he sent a fleet and chased the intruders out of the area.

In 1589, when Mirale Bey arrived with a fleet of five ships on his second heavy raid, the viceroy again sent a fleet from Goa to protect Portugal's precariously exercised rule. Mirale Bey was badly outgunned, and could not hope to hold out against the Portuguese.

Also, soon after the Portuguese galleons appeared on the horizon, a horde of migratory cannibals began gathering in strength on the mainland opposite Mombasa. These were the

Zimba, a Bantu tribe from the Zambezi River; they had been eating their way up the coast, and had devoured the settlement at Kilwa. The Sultan of Mombasa pleaded with Mirale Bey for protection, and the Turk sent two of his five ships around the island to keep an eye on the cannibals.

The Portuguese captured the three Turkish ships waiting for them in deep water. Then the Portuguese sank the two ships standing watch at the ford. When the Portuguese anchored offshore, the Zimba swarmed across the ford and onto the island, making a feast of everyone they could find.

After the Zimba left Mombasa they continued northward to Malindi, but were successfully resisted there. Tradition in Malindi holds that the Zimba were also attacked from behind by the Segeju, another Bantu tribe. In any case, the fog of history swallowed the Zimba at the end of one of the cruelest and most carnivorous of all human migrations.

When the Portuguese again had serious trouble from Mombasa, in 1592, they deposed the sultan and put the Sultan of Malindi in charge of the place.

The construction of Fort Jesus was started the next year at the entrance to the old harbor, on a high ridge of coral, at a point where ships are forced close to shore by shoals and the currents of the channel. The coral was cut back to create a vertical face below the fort's own thick walls. Every wall was covered by a protecting bastion. On the harbor side there was a projecting gun platform with a wide field of fire. On the approach from the island there was a deep ditch, and then an overhanging shelter at the fort where the townspeople could find safety when Mombasa was being bombarded.

Within a couple of years most of the masonry was up, although it took decades to really finish the famous fort, called the Fort of Jesus at Mombasa. It remained impregnable for nearly three hundred years, and was not surrendered by men in fighting condition until it was bombarded by rockets and shells from British warships in 1875.

The fort changed hands occasionally, but only when the garrison was starved into submission, or fell to diseases while it was under siege, or when it was deceived or surprised by people inside, as were the Portuguese after they proclaimed Yusuf bin Hasan the sultan.

Yusuf had been sent to Goa to study. He had become a Christian with the new name of Don Geronimo Chingulia, and took a young Goan as his bride. In Mombasa, the Arabs and Swahilis were Moslems, and seemed not to approve of his conversion to Christianity or of his Christian bride.

In 1631, five years after Don Geronimo assumed the sultanate, a spy saw him chanting a prayer at his father's tomb in the Moslem way. The spy reported this to the Portuguese captain, and on the same night warned Don Geronimo of what he had done, presumably expecting double payment for his efforts.

The young sultan had his informer killed, and then went the next morning to the chapel of the fort, where the Portuguese officers were celebrating the Feast of the Assumption of the Virgin Mary. When the commander of the fort, Pedro de Gamboa, rose to meet his visitor, he was stabbed to death by Don Geronimo. His three hundred followers fell on the others and within minutes had put nearly all the Portuguese in Mombasa to death. One Portuguese who renounced his Christianity was spared. Five others escaped to the Bajun Islands in a canoe. The rest of the garrison of a hundred men and an unknown number of civilians were killed. Don Geronimo reverted to the name Yusuf and openly returned to Islam.

Yusuf held Mombasa for a year. The Portuguese sent a fleet from Goa to dislodge him. It failed in its first attempt, but Yusuf saw that he could not hold out against another. The people of Mombasa were still too suspicious and resentful of him to give him their full support. He captured a Portuguese galleon and took to piracy in the Red Sea with a few loyal followers, and died in 1638, a bitter man.

In Mombasa the Portuguese resumed their shaky hegemony. The Arabs from the Persian Gulf were again threatening the coast, fomenting rebellion where they could, and sacking towns that remained loyal to the Portuguese, but insufficiently protected.

Real trouble came on gradually, after March 13, 1696, when

a large Arab fleet from Oman laid siege to Fort Jesus. Portuguese reinforcements were slipped in easily at first through the Arabs' ships. Food could still be got on the mainland. The Queen of Zanzibar sent help for her Portuguese allies.

By July 1697 the privation was terrible. The Portuguese defenders had been reduced by disease and starvation to the fort commander, a priest and two soldiers. They were supported by the loyal Swahili chief, Bwana Daud, with about thirty Swahili followers and forty African women who fought no less bravely than the men. In beating off an attack on July 20, the African women carried a dying Portuguese soldier to his swivel gun that he might fire it again before he died. The women pushed scaling ladders away from the walls and threw grenades into the mass of Arabs below.

Within the next week the priest and the last two soldiers were dead. Four days later the fort commander died, leaving Bwana Daud in charge of the fort. He held out against the Arabs until a Portuguese relief expedition landed men and stores in October. In December another Portuguese commander arrived and was so little liked by Bwana Daud and the Swahilis that they refused to stay, and were evacuated to Goa.

They barely made it away, for on December 13, with the garrison reduced to eight Portuguese, three Indians and two African women, the Arabs launched a massive and successful attack at night. The new commander rushed into the attacking Arabs, firing his blunderbuss before he fell. Two of the Portuguese soldiers led a crowd of Arabs into the powder magazine, telling them it contained a hoard of gold. When the magazine was packed with people, the Portuguese blew it up, with themselves and everyone else in the place. The siege had lasted thirty-three months, and had cost eight hundred Portuguese and three thousand Swahilis their lives, mostly from fever and plague.

The Portuguese interest in Mombasa had been dwindling for a long time, and this contributed to their unwillingness to fight a real war to keep it. Mombasa's trade importance had been falling off. Ships were sailing for India from Mozambique, an ideal place to start out on the monsoon when it was blowing the right way. By the end of the seventeenth century, Dutch and English ships were beginning to appear increasingly in the Indian Ocean.

With Mombasa lost to the Arabs, the Portuguese were driven out of Kilwa and Pemba by them a year later. The Portuguese reoccupied the Mombasa fort in 1728, but were defeated again and forced to evacuate after only 18 months in possession. There was one more unsuccessful attempt by the Portuguese to capture the fort, in 1769, but they failed to dislodge the Arabs.

The Portuguese, north of Mozambique, were a spent force in East Africa. The overlordship of the coast as far south as Cape Delgado passed from Portugal to the Omani Sultanate. The Omani Arabs stuck to the island fortresses, and were no more able to exercise direct rule than the Portuguese had been. Real power for the Arabs was to be shorter and more limited than before.

Like the Arabs, the Portuguese had acquired some knowledge of the interior, mainly from trading caravans. Neither the Arabs nor the Portuguese nor the Indian traders who made their way to the East African coast showed much desire to explore the vast continent which lay behind the coast.

They were seafarers and merchants. They were content to exchange their beads, glass, metal objects and cloth and sometimes guns for ivory, ambergris, slaves and gold.

There were no navigable rivers on which to penetrate the interior. Travel was a slow and hazardous affair. Beyond the mangrove swamps there were hostile tribes and diseases and a host of natural barriers. From the other side of the continent, travel was hindered by thick, impenetrable forests. In the north was the great barrier of the desert.

The vast grasslands and cool forests of East Africa were isolated and known only to the people who lived there. Despite the great discoveries on other continents by the end of the eighteenth century, East Africa remained much as Jonathan Swift has described it:

> So geographers, in Afric-maps,
> With savage pictures fill their gaps;
> And o'er unhabitable downs,
> Place elephants for want of towns.

# CHAPTER 3

# THE IMPACT
# OF THE WEST

Europe had for a very long time been fascinated by the mysteries of Africa. Little was known, and little was believed of the stories carried abroad by traders and sailors, about snow-clad mountains at the Equator, or about the great lakes that fed the Nile.

From Europe people went to East Africa for a variety of reasons: some to explore, some to save pagan souls, some to trade in slaves and some to suppress the slave trade, some eventually to settle. The British came partly to find and control the sources of the Nile, so that they could protect their positions in Egypt and the Sudan. The Germans came at first as missionaries and explorers, but were soon trying to catch up in the scramble for markets and concessions and colonial territory. It took the Europeans a long time to discern what their real interests were; the Uganda Railroad was built by the British with scant thought of the development of the land that was to become known as Kenya. It was then no more than a corridor to Uganda.

Slavery and the foreign penetration of the continent left in-

delible marks in East Africa's history, even though Africans were
at the source of the trade. Weak tribes were preyed on by the
stronger, more warlike ones: the Yao in the south, the Wanyamwezi and the Baganda around the great lakes, and others. The
Africans sold their captives to the Arabs, often in exchange for
guns and gunpowder.

The demand for slaves rose with the growth of the huge sugar
plantations in Mauritius and the West Indies, and the coffee
plantations and the cotton and tobacco fields in the Americas.

As the slave trade grew, so did the suffering that was endured
on the slave caravans, some of them with hundreds of men,
women and children manacled one to the next, or each with his
neck imprisoned in a forked stick that was tied to another on the
person in front of him. Sometimes the slaves marched hundreds
of miles to the coast, carrying ivory and other things on their
heads, their necks chafed and bleeding, their backs showing the
marks of being whipped to a quicker pace.

At the height of the slave trade, at the end of the eighteenth
century, close to twenty thousand slaves were being brought each
year from the interior of Africa to the slave market in Zanzibar
alone. Perhaps ten million people were captured and sold by
slavers in East Africa.

The slave trails converged until they became well-traveled
roads to the coast, ending at places opposite Zanzibar or Kilwa
or Lamu. Some slave routes led northward to the Nile and down
the river to Khartoum. But mainly they lay across what was to
become Tanzania, and led to the towns opposite Zanzibar Island,
to such places as Sadani and Pangani and Bagamoyo. The last
of these was the most notorious. Bagamoyo was given its name
by the slaves who passed through it, not knowing where they were
going, knowing only that they were not coming back. It means
"throw away your heart."

The excesses and the magnitude of the slave trade eventually
stirred the people in Europe to oppose it vigorously, and to
raise campaigns against it. The agitation in England rose until
the slave trade was finally abolished in 1807 in British-controlled
territories.

*A slave caravan on its way to the coast*

In East African waters, however, the British effort was not so quick and thorough as it was along the West African coast. In 1798 Britain had made a treaty of friendship with the Imam of Oman, the ruler of the desert land on the Arabian peninsula. The Imam needed help from wherever he could get it to maintain control of his dominions on the East coast of Africa, and to give him some authority in the unending quarrels and intrigues among the local Arab clans that had been left to rule these places. Britain needed a pretext to tighten her foothold in the area. As Oman's main trade was in slaves, the British moved slowly against it, so as not to antagonize their ally.

A compromise between Oman and Britain was reached in 1822, with a treaty limiting the slave trade to the western half of the Indian Ocean, to prevent slaves being imported into India.

Five years later a second slavery treaty limited the trade to

Oman's African possessions, but still the violations went almost unchecked and the slave trade lingered.

Oman's difficulties in controlling her African possessions dragged on, too. But with recognition and the expectation of assistance from Britain the Omani ruler, who styled himself Sultan Seyyid Said bin Sultan, sailed with a fleet to Zanzibar and used the island as a base from which to reassert his authority on the East African coast. In 1822 he drove a rebellious ruling clan of Arabs from Zanzibar's sister island of Pemba. Four years later the sultan forced the same clan out of power in Mombasa.

During the campaign and in the years immediately afterward, the sultan grew to like Zanzibar so much he moved his capital there. Unlike his dusty old capital of Muscat, Zanzibar was green. It had plenty of sweet water and a pleasant, balmy climate. The sultan planted cloves from the Moluccas, and this sweet-smelling spice was to become the mainstay of the island's economy. Seyyid Said died at sea in 1856, but for the rest of the century Zanzibar town was the capital of this wobbly, widespread empire.

Zanzibar's influence on the coast had been kept intact by external forces, mainly by British gunboats and British diplomacy. Much of the slave trade was financed by Indians who settled on Zanzibar and the coast. They claimed British protection and imported British goods. Because they also paid a heavy tax to the sultan, he accepted them. In 1875, when Mombasa again rebelled, this time against Sultan Barghash, British warships came to his help and shelled Fort Jesus from the sea for over half an hour before the commandant surrendered.

The sultan's rule extended even less inland, despite the commercial influence of Zanzibar along the caravan routes. The number of Arabs in the interior was probably never more than a few hundred, and the number of Swahili people perhaps one or two thousand. Both had established themselves in the interior as merchants, selling by barter to the Africans. But it was chiefly the widening European interest that altered East Africa, and not the Arabs. It was the adventurers, the missionaries and merchants and empire builders from Europe who left the greater impact on the place, many of them attracted by legends that were thousands of years old.

From early times there had been stories of great lakes and snow-capped mountains deep in Africa. Ptolemy, the Alexandrian geographer, wrote an account in the second century A.D. of how Diogenes, a Greek trader, five centuries earlier, had "landed at Rhaptum, journeyed inland for twenty-five days, and arrived in the vicinity of the two great lakes and the snowy range of mountains whence the Nile draws its twin sources." The legend of high twin peaks at the Nile source was mentioned in the fifth century B.C. by Herodotus, who called the peaks Crophi and Mophi. Yet when the first reports reached England in the nineteenth century from Europeans who had seen snow-covered mountains, they were flatly disbelieved.

The first missionary explorer in East Africa was Ludwig Krapf, a German missionary who abandoned his work among the Galla in Ethiopia as hopeless, and sailed for Zanzibar to ask the sultan's permission to open a mission in his territory. On the way, Dr. Krapf's dhow called at Takaungu, where he was told about a great mountain known by the Chagga as *Kilimanjaro*. The missionary was also told about a "great sea beyond the country Uniamuezi" and his interest in exploration was aroused.

With the Sultan's consent, Krapf set up his new mission at Rabai Mpia, near Mombasa. His wife and baby daughter died of malaria there within a few weeks of their landing, and Krapf threw himself into his missionary work with fervor, completing a translation of the New Testament into Swahili in five months.

In 1846 he was joined at Rabai by Johann Rebmann and the two journeyed often into the interior, although neither seemed cut out to be an explorer. Rebmann was very nearsighted, and was said to have been rescued more than once from rhinos he never saw, although they were charging him head-on. Krapf was hopelessly clumsy and unlucky, his pack animals often running away, or his muzzle-loading gun getting jammed or going off at the wrong time. When he was told to use the gun once against a raiding party of Africans, he fired into the trees rather than risk hurting anyone, even though spears were being hurled at him. His secret weapon was the umbrella he slept under at night. On a journey with the Kamba chief Kivoi to see the Tana River, Krapf wrote of how his umbrella had been opened abruptly to frighten away some raiders:

"In the confusions and hurry of loading I had left my ramrod in the barrel of my gun, and fired it off, so that I could not load again. Whilst we were firing, and our caravan was preparing for a conflict, Kivoi ordered one of his wives to open my umbrella, when the robbers immediately slackened their speed."

The nearsighted Rebmann was the first European to see Kilimanjaro. On the morning of May 11, 1848, on a visit to the Chagga tribe, the missionary peered ahead excitedly at the slopes he had seen rising from the Masai plain. He wrote:

"This morning we discerned the mountains of Jagga more distinctly than ever; at about ten o'clock, I fancied I saw the summit of one of them covered with a dazzlingly white cloud. My guide called the white which I saw, merely '*Beredi,*' cold; it was perfectly clear to me, however, that it could be nothing else but snow."

On December 3, 1849, Krapf, traveling northeast from Rabai toward Kitui and the Kamba country, was shown Mount Kenya by Chief Kivoi. The Kamba called it *Kima ja Kegnia,* the "Mountain of Whiteness."

In 1857, nearly a decade later, the explorers Richard Burton and John Hanning Speke were led by an Arab caravan to Tabora where they learned there were three great lakes in the interior.

The flamboyant Burton and the quiet, determined Speke had already explored together in Somalia, and quarreled constantly. Yet that did not prevent them from starting this new venture.

At Tabora, Burton was too weak with fever and dysentery to go on, and Speke continued alone to Lake Victoria. He returned to tell Burton he was certain he had found the main source of the Nile, but Burton scoffed at the idea and the two had something new to quarrel about on their long journey back from Tabora.

Speke went again with Captain J. A. Grant. These two left

Zanzibar in October 1860, and traveled around the western shore of the lake to Karagwe, where Grant became too sick to go on. Speke went ahead without him, eventually to a cataract over which a mighty river left Lake Victoria. The venture had taken nearly two years and there was no doubt in Speke's mind that this was the White Nile.

It had been known even by Ptolemy that there were two rivers, a Blue Nile and a White Nile, and that they flowed together at Khartoum before crossing into Egypt and to the sea. The White Nile is the longer, slower moving river, emerging not precisely white but as a winding, muddy gray ribbon out of the fetid, mauve-green sea of reeds in the southern Sudan. The Blue Nile is rarely very blue, and for half a year it rushes out of the Ethiopian mountains in a reddish-brown flood with such force that the White Nile is dammed back upon itself at Khartoum, unable to flow easily into its rushing sister river.

The source of the Blue Nile was found in 1770 at Lake Tana, in Ethiopia, by James Bruce, the Scottish explorer. It remained for Speke, on July 28, 1862, to find the main source of the White Nile at Lake Victoria. For Europe it was a thrilling discovery, but the place was hardly an unknown wilderness, as Speke made clear when he described the scene at Ripon Falls:

"It was a sight that attracted one to it for hours," he wrote. "The roar of the waters, the thousands of passenger-fish, leaping at the falls with all their might; the Wasoga and Waganda fishermen coming out in boats and taking post on all the rocks with rod and hook, hippopotami and crocodiles lying sleeping at the water, the ferry at work above the falls, and cattle driven down to drink at the margin of the lake—made in all, with the pretty nature of the country—small hills, grassy topped, with trees in the folds, and gardens on the lower slopes—as interesting a picture as one could wish to see."

David Livingstone, with long experience as a missionary and explorer in Africa, was commissioned to clear up doubts that remained about Speke's report; Livingstone was convinced that the Nile rose to the south of Lake Victoria. Other arguments

persist even today: melting snows from the Ruwenzori Mountains flow eventually into the Nile, and the Kagera River flows
into Lake Victoria from the west. But this is an academic con-
troversy and neither the Ruwenzori Mountains nor the Kagera
River is generally regarded as the source of the White Nile; the
source is Lake Victoria, as Speke had believed, although the
roar of waters at Ripon Falls is gone now, submerged by the
ponding back of water from a dam the British built much later,
farther down the river at Owen Falls.

Livingstone pursued his own theory, however, and reached
Ujiji in March 1869, setting out from there to explore the Nile
and Congo river systems. In October he crossed back to Ujiji,
exhausted and out of supplies, unable either to continue his
exploration or to head back for the coast. The *New York Herald*
had presumed Livingstone to be lost, and commissioned Henry
Morton Stanley to look for him. Stanley succeeded in finding
him in November, greeting him with the historic salutation "Dr.
Livingstone, I presume."

Stanley sailed around Lake Victoria then, settling the questions
of its size and nature. He explored the land between Lake Edward
and Victoria, surveyed Lake Tanganyika, traced the course of the
Congo, crossed the Ituri Forest and came upon the towering
presence of the Ruwenzori Mountains, the "Mountains of the
Moon."

Together, Stanley and Livingstone explored Lake Victoria, and
then Stanley started back, leaving Livingstone to regain his
strength and continue his study of the Nile and Congo river systems, as he had wanted. But Livingstone weakened again and
had to be carried on a litter. On April 17, 1873, after his arrival
in Chitambo's village near Lake Bangweulu, he made the last
entry in his journal, writing that he felt "knocked up quite." On
May 1 his servants found him dead.

In spite of the taboos in Africa about the dead, his servants
preserved his body and carried it six hundred miles back to the
coast, eventually to be buried in Westminster Abbey in London.
The last of his group of devoted Africans died in Mombasa in

*Stanley and his party in East Africa*

1935 and was buried in the shade of the mango and kapok trees
at Kisauni.

Livingstone's death ended a classic period of African exploration. His writings had spurred the missionary and exploratory
zeal of the British, and the quest for colonial territory.

German colonialism in East Africa was stirred by the arrival
in 1884 of Carl Peters, a resolute young man who ventured up
the Wami River, signing treaties with African chiefs and establishing a German interest in what was to become Tanganyika. With
his treaties as proof of German influence, Peters returned to Berlin and founded the German East Africa Company. He trans-

ferred the treaties to it, and then persuaded Otto von Bismarck, the "Iron Chancellor," to declare the area a German protectorate.

The Sultan of Zanzibar protested to the British against this unwanted German protection for part of his territory. The British East Africa Company also protested, for it had treaties with some of the same chiefs who had made treaties with the Germans.

The sultan even sent some of his troops to the slopes of Kilimanjaro to persuade Chief Mandara of the Chagga to renounce his treaty with the Germans, and reaffirm his treaty with the British and his loyalty to the sultan.

Chief Mandara did this, but when the Germans returned with more troops, he speedily changed his mind again, ceding all his lands and his sovereignty to the German East Africa Company.

Even the sultan, Seyyid Barghash, had to accept that power flowed from the barrel of a gun. In August 1885, a squadron of German warships dropped anchor off Zanzibar, and presented the sultan with a treaty to sign, accepting the German protectorate behind a coastal strip of land, ten miles wide, where the sultan was recognized as sovereign.

The sultan hesitated only long enough to see the Germans start to clear their decks for action. Then he signed. So that the Germans would have a port to serve their protectorate, the sultan also ceded Dar es Salaam.

In 1886 and 1890 the British and Germans agreed on the limits of the sultan's nominal sovereignty, and extended the ten-mile-wide coastal strip northward into Britain's sphere of interest to Kipini at the mouth of the Tana River. Not even this added to the sultan's real authority; it served only to remove the German trading company from the Tana River area, for the coastal strip in the north was placed under British protection. For all practical purposes, the sultan's coastal property in the south was handed to the Germans.

The sultan accepted, for he was an old and very sick man then, and had no choice. At Tanga, Pangani and Bagamoyo, however, the Arabs and Swahili rioted when they saw the German flag flying alongside the plain red banner of the sultan, then Seyyid Khalifa, who succeeded his brother Barghash in April 1888.

A Zanzibar Arab, Bushiri bin Salim, led a brief rebellion against the Germans in the mainland settlements close to the coast. He attacked Dar es Salaam unsuccessfully, but he captured Kilwa and forced the Germans to evacuate Mikindani, Lindi and the settlements around Tanga and Pangani. When Moshi and Arusha in the northeastern highlands were threatened, the German government took over from the company, retook Pangani and Tanga, defeated Bushiri's forces twice near Bagamoyo and finally captured Bushiri himself. He was taken to Pangani and hanged on December 15, 1889.

In the southern highlands the Hehe were also stirred to revolt, and in 1894 the Germans stormed the walled village of Kalenga where the Hehe chief, Mkwawa, held court. He escaped and the Germans tracked him for four years before they found him. Then the chief shot himself rather than be taken alive.

There were also expeditions against the Wanyamwezi, the Wagogo and the Wajiji. Smaller operations to keep the tribes at peace were carried out for twelve years until 1903, when the country seemed quiet. But it was a deceptive quiet.

Resentment against the Germans smoldered for many reasons, including the taking of land for white settlement or for big plantations, the demands on tribal chiefs that they recruit workers for the plantations and especially the hut tax levied by the German authorities.

By 1905 the feeling of rebellion had spread widely and was strongest among the tribes south of the Rufiji River, the center of a snake cult that believed their witch doctors could compound a liquid that would give them immunity from German bullets, and turn the bullets to water.

*Maji* is Swahili for water. Maji Maji became the name of the smoldering rebellion, with the word doubled for emphasis, as is normal in the language, and as the British were to learn much later in Kenya with the Mau Mau rebellion there.

The trouble broke into the open at a government cotton farm at Kibata, near Kilwa, on the night of July 31, 1905. The workers marched on the small town of Samanga and set it afire. The rebellion then spread through the Rufiji River Basin, over the

Mahenge Plateau and into the Lukuledi and Kilombero valleys. Officials, planters, missionaries and other Germans were taken by surprise in their missions and settlements over the whole southern part of the country, and murdered.

On August 30 more than eight thousand Mbunga and Pogoro tribesmen attacked Mahenge, but the Germans repulsed the attack, inflicting heavy casualties with machine-gun bullets that did not turn to water.

By November the worst of the rebellion was over, but the few Africans who held out were elusive and the populace was hostile or frightened of reprisal by one side or the other. In 1907 Abdullah Mpanda, one of the leaders of the uprising, was killed

*Ivory traders in German East Africa*

and the last resistance collapsed, but not until many villages and crops had been destroyed. In the famine that followed, more than one hundred thousand Africans died, mainly from starvation.

The British were still establishing their authority, too. The British East Africa Association became the Imperial British East Africa Company, with authority to administer as much of the British sphere of influence as it could obtain treaties over. One of the company's nagging problems, however, was the rich Kingdom of Buganda. Traders and missionaries were having trouble with the king, Kabaka Mwanga, and he was having trouble with a band of rebellious Moslems in his kingdom.

The Kabaka sent out a call to the British for help. Carl Peters, the bold young German, intercepted it and, sensing an opportunity to extend Germany's influence, headed for Buganda.

He started out into the British sphere of influence with fewer than fifty men, a mere tenth of the mighty caravans that normally set out for the interior. Peters sailed from Zanzibar in June 1889, slipped past a blockade of two British warships, and started up the Tana River. He fought some fierce battles with unfriendly tribes, including the Masai; this enabled him, on his arrival at Lake Baringo, to offer protection to the Wakuafi, traditional enemies of the Masai.

Peters raised the German flag at Njemps on January 8, 1890, and reported to the German government that "a Baringo nation would be one of the very greatest importance for the general opening up of Central Africa."

While the authorities in Berlin were presumably pondering the usefulness of this remote and undefined new acquisition, Peters arrived in Buganda and signed a treaty with the Kabaka, placing Buganda in the German sphere of influence, too. Peters then heard that a British party of more than five hundred was heading for Buganda, not only to help Kabaka Mwanga out of trouble, but to challenge Peters and his new treaty. Peters asked the Somali if they would fight. When they showed their reluctance, Peters left.

His personal defeat in Buganda was of no consequence to East Africa, for Germany and Britain were making their own, wider-reaching agreements, in the Act of Brussels in July 1890, ratifying the boundaries already fixed. The tiny island of Heligoland in the North Sea was handed to Germany for the recognition of Zanzibar, Pemba and Witu as British protectorates.

Peters realized that his expedition and his treaties had been rendered useless. At Bagamoyo, he was taken aside by a friend and told of the Brussels agreement.

"I will pass in silence over the emotions these tidings excited in me," Peters wrote in his journal afterward. "I remained two hours in the salon to regain my composure, and begged the gentlemen to say nothing more on the whole subject."

The missionaries continued to have their problems in Buganda. They had concentrated their efforts at first in Buganda because of its highly developed court and administration, the relative ease of living there, and the quickness with which the Baganda responded to their teaching.

Because of this, Kabaka Mwanga suspected the missionaries of working against him. He resented their preachings about the immorality of his court. He resented the young men who went to the missionaries to "read," that is, to be instructed in Christianity.

Because he was suspicious and wanted to keep the missionaries in close check, the Kabaka kept them near him. Therefore most of the converts to Christianity were among the influential young men who served as pages or were otherwise part of the court.

Mwanga sensed that his position was being weakened among the families of substance and position; in an attempt to discourage the young men, he ordered three young Protestants dismembered and burned on January 31, 1885. Within two years, twenty more Protestants and twenty-two Catholics had been killed. Hundreds more were put to death in nearby villages.

The young Christians who survived fled to the forests where they persuaded others to become Christians, too, and the insurrection against Mwanga gathered momentum.

Although Mwanga had himself been converted to Islam, the Moslems also turned against him when they learned he was planning to do away with all the Moslems and Christians in the kingdom by leaving them stranded on an island in Lake Victoria.

The man who gave away the plan was Apolo Kagwa, the Kabaka's *Katikkiro,* or prime minister. Apolo Kagwa was a pagan. Moslems, Catholics, Protestants and pagans stopped fighting among themselves long enough then to join forces against the Kabaka and drive him from the country in 1888.

But afterward the Moslems, with help from the Arabs, turned on the Christians. They fled, but returned with Mwanga and restored him to the throne, drove the Moslems away, and divided power among themselves.

The Moslems in Buganda had always been identified with the Arabs, and helped by them. Because of the nationalities of the first missionaries in Buganda, the Catholics among the Baganda were known as *Bafalansa,* or French, and the Baganda Protestants were known as *Bangereza,* or English. The Baganda converts tended to think of themselves in terms of European power politics.

Even after independence a commonly heard phrase in Kampala at election time was "*Ssi muganda mukatoliki,*" meaning "He's not a Muganda; he's a Catholic."

During Kabaka Mwanga's second reign, the British were able to consolidate their authority in Buganda. They intervened frequently to get Protestant Baganda into positions of influence, in spite of their relatively small numbers. When enough of the younger generation of chiefs and administrative leaders seemed to favor Britain, the way was open for her to make Buganda the terminal of the railroad into the interior.

The British government took over from the British East Africa Company on July 1, 1895, and declared a protectorate over the whole of what was to become Kenya and Uganda.

In the same year the British government invited the British Catholic Mill Hill Mission to enter Buganda, to dilute the influence over Baganda Catholics enjoyed by the White Fathers, who were mostly French.

When Mwanga tried to rebel in 1897 he was deposed by the British who put his one-year-old son, Daudi Chwa, on the throne as Kabaka, with Apolo Kagwa as regent to manage the affairs of

*Mwanga, King of Uganda, about 1893*

state for the infant. Apolo Kagwa signed an agreement with the British in 1900 to cement his cooperation. It was followed by similar agreements in Toro and Ankole to the west, and helped lead the Baganda to their long period of dominance among the Africans in the Uganda territory.

The starting point of the British railroad line on the coast was to be Mombasa, an appropriate place, not only because of its fine, natural harbor, but because the name was derived from the Arabic word *Mimbashia* which means "the country which unfolds itself." The line was to run to Kavirondo Gulf, on Lake Victoria. The traffic was to go from there by steamer to Uganda.

In his book *Facing Mount Kenya*, Jomo Kenyatta relates how Mogo wa Kebiro, a famous Kikuyu witch doctor, had foretold the coming of men of the same pale color as the *kiengere* frog, with sticks that would spit deadly fire, and with an iron snake that would extend all the way from the Indian Ocean to Lake Victoria.

Because Africans shied away from the railroad construction or could not be easily trained to it, nearly all the labor force of more than thirty thousand was recruited in India, including tradesmen, craftsmen, clerks and coolies. Most of them stayed when the railroad was completed, and many sent for their relatives and friends, settling in the towns along the line of rail, or opening the shops known as *dukas,* to barter and sell to both Africans and white men. The Indian shopkeeper, or *duka-wallah,* remained a prominent and pervasive part of the East Africa landscape.

One of the names on the line of rail remains from the time when Indians worked on it: the Athi River Station. The name is believed to have come from the Punjabi artisans who saw hippopotamuses submerged in the river there, and cried out: *"Hathi! Hathi!"* meaning "Elephants!" The Punjabis knew nothing of hippos.

Serious problems were encountered in the construction of the railroad. There were no roads apart from the elephant trails and the converging paths left by slave caravans. The building materials had to be transported by camels and donkeys and sometimes on the heads of porters.

The man-eating lions of Tsavo ate scores of Indians and brought construction to a standstill for a few months in 1898. At Kima, then a barren wilderness, and eventually a center for the sisal industry, a lion climbed into a railroad car and carried off the superintendent of railroad police. Another time at Kima, a lion jumped onto the station and began tearing at the corrugated iron sheets of the roof to get at the Indian telegraph operator below. The terrified man sent this message back down the line: "Lion fighting with station. Send urgent succour."

In May 1899, the line reached *Uaso N'airobi,* the place where a cold stream ran through a pleasant swamp and into a plain which the Masai called *Nakuso-Ntelon,* meaning "the beginning of all beauty." The depot and workshops were set up in the encampment that was eventually to grow into the city of Nairobi.

From there the route continued down the Rift Valley escarpment, across the valley floor past the crusted lakes of boiling mud, past the scattered cones of extinct volcanoes, then up through the highlands and down again to the shore of Lake Victoria at Kisumu in December 1901. The whole project had taken six years.

Stanley had seen Kisumu in March 1897 when he sailed around the lake to Kavirondo Gulf, but he had seen no sign of life in the abandoned settlement. The name is either a corruption of a Nilotic word meaning "a hungry place" or Swahili meaning "the place of the knife," possibly because it had been a battleground for tribes around the lake.

Within half a dozen years, however, it had become a thriving place, with a market and many small *dukas* and workshops that Indians had set up. White men came up the line of rail, too, as administrators and businessmen. Missionaries came in greater numbers, and with their families. Some white men came to clear farms out of the bush, and to settle.

To the Bantu Africans, all white men were deemed to be of one race. All were called Bazungu or Wazungu, depending on the Bantu language. One young Muganda boy named Mwana Awulira, who was later converted to Christianity, marveled at how the missionaries ate their meals off a large wooden board with legs, at how they used tools to eat with instead of their hands alone and at the way they sang after they had eaten.

"I have never heard singing like that before, and I did not like it much," the boy said later. "Then they stopped and everyone knelt down, and I did too, and the Bazungu began to say words, praying to someone, some great chief, but I could see no one but ourselves. My mistress then told me I was to stay there. I did not mind for there were other boys, and I soon got used to the new life."

In Kamba country, a missionary's wife marveled at the way the Africans studied them on their arrival and were particularly amused at the long straight hair of her children. She wrote: "They would say to one another *'Tazama! Tazama! Nzii yake ta kisithi kya n'gatata!'* (Look! Look! Her hair is like a gnu's tail!)"

When World War I broke out in 1914, there were few troops

on either the British or German side of their common border in East Africa, which remained where it had been set by the agreements of 1886 and 1890: from the mouth of the Umba River to the northern foothills of Kilimanjaro, then in a straight line to Lake Victoria, and then westward to the Congo border.

For the Germans the outlook was grim; there were enemies on all sides. To the north, in what was to become Kenya and Uganda, were the British. To the west, beyond Lake Kivu and Lake Tanganyika and the German-occupied kingdoms of Rwanda and Burundi, were the Belgians in the Congo. To the south, beyond the southern highlands and Lake Nyasa, in territories that were to become Zambia and Malawi, were the British again. East of them, on the other side of the Ruvuma River, were the Portuguese in Mozambique.

The Germans had only the advantage of a gifted and experienced military leader, General Paul von Lettow-Vorbeck. He had garrisons to man, and warring tribes to keep under control. He also knew that no action in East Africa could be decisive in a European war, but he fought to harass the British troops and tied them down as best he could.

The Germans' cruiser, the *Königsberg*, was outnumbered by three British cruisers: the *Astrea, Hyacinth* and *Pegasus.* Yet the *Königsberg* managed to raid British shipping, bombard Zanzibar and sink the *Pegasus.* When she ran short of fuel, the *Königsberg* retreated up the Rufiji River where the heavier British cruisers, with their deeper draft, could not follow her. She was blockaded for nearly a year before two British gunboats with high-trajectory guns sailed out from London and sank her.

Von Lettow-Vorbeck concentrated his forces around Kilimanjaro, where there was food and where he could find hiding places from which to make raids across the border, cutting the railroad line many times and capturing the frontier town of Taveta.

The British tried to capture Tanga but were beaten back. A British column advancing around Kilimanjaro to take the Germans from behind was routed. The Germans captured Jassini, but only because von Lettow-Vorbeck was hoping to draw British reinforcements to the attack. When they did not come, he withdrew to Kilimanjaro to continue his harassment of the railroad line.

By 1916 Indian and South African troops under the command of the Boer General Jan Christian Smuts joined in the pursuit of von Lettow-Vorbeck, but he proved too elusive. The Belgians crossed from the Congo and joined with the British to capture Mwanza, but the German general ignored the fringe engagements.

He concentrated on harassing Smuts and the British, fighting a nuisance war, standing his ground only when it was high and favorable. Finally he withdrew into Portuguese East Africa, and struck from there into British territory in what was to become Zambia.

On November 25, 1918, two weeks after the armistice in Europe, General von Lettow-Vorbeck formally capitulated at Abercorn. His total force consisted of 155 Germans and other Europeans and 4,227 Africans, of whom 819 were women, and the rest were trained soldiers, known in East Africa as *askaris*.

This ragged army had never been more than three hundred Germans and eleven thousand Africans, according to the German general. Yet with this poorly fed, poorly armed force, he had pinned down a British army that finally put 137 generals and three hundred thousand men in the field, including British, South African, Rhodesian, Indian and African troops, not only from East Africa but from Nigeria and elsewhere on the continent.

Before he died in Hamburg on March 9, 1964, at the age of ninety-four, General von Lettow-Vorbeck was much celebrated for his skill and daring in the war. General Smuts helped organize a testimonial dinner for him in London in 1929. At the time of his capitulation, the *Bulawayo Chronicle* reflected the admiration the British in Africa had for the man and his defiant army even then:

"Von Lettow, whose striking presence is a good index of what must be a wonderful personality, came in at the head of his first detachment . . . It was a most impressive spectacle. The long motley column, Europeans and Askaris, all veterans of a hundred fights, the latter clothed in every kind of headgear, women who had stuck to their husbands through all these years of hardship, carrying huge loads, some with children born during the campaign, carriers coming in singing in undisguised joy at the thought that their labors were ended at last."

Except for the western kingdoms of Rwanda and Burundi, which were turned over to Belgium after the war, the British were given a mandate by the League of Nations to govern the German territory. It was named for Lake Tanganyika, a compound of two Swahili words: *tanga*, a sail, and *nyika*, a plateau.

In 1920 Kenya took its name from its principal mountain. The ten-mile strip of coast from Lamu to the Tanganyika border, territory that had belonged nominally to the Sultan of Zanzibar, was added to Kenya and the sultan was paid an annual rent for it.

World War I had been a turning point in East African history. The spectacle of two European tribes at war with each other dealt an irreparable blow to the white man's mystique. Much of the land, especially in Kenya, had been set aside earlier for white settlement. It was inevitable that the Africans would agitate eventually to have it back.

# CHAPTER 4

# THE RISE OF NATIONALISM:

# KENYA AND TANZANIA

When Jomo Kenyatta was a boy in Ichaweri, he used to herd cattle on the pasture around Mogumo-wa-Njathi, the only sacred tree left in his neighborhood. There were other trees around, but this was the only one left where ancestor-spirits could reside: the white settlers, in clearing their newly acquired plots for cultivation, had cut down all the sacred trees except Mogumo-wa-Njathi. It was the only tree around Ichaweri where the Kikuyu could make sacrifices for rain, or where communion of any sort could be had with Ngai, the Divider of the Universe.

People would go to the tree and lament: *"Gikuyu harea keari kianoimaho,"* meaning "the Kikuyu are no longer where they used to be." The restless, hot-tempered little cowherd would sometimes run from the pasture in anger and shame for his tribe, and wonder how long Ngai, sitting up there on his resting place atop Mount Kenya, would put up with the intruding whites.

For half a century a proportion of this fertile highland area was reserved for white settlement; the area was known until independence as the "white highlands," and eventually took up a fifth

*A farmer in a Kikuyu village*

of Kenya's good farming land. Before independence, whites owned more than thirty-five hundred farms in Kenya, including 550 big plantations on which coffee, tea and other valuable crops were grown. The whites who settled in Kenya outnumbered by far the whites who settled in Tanzania and Uganda. Their farms were the mainstay of Kenya's economy, producing four times as much marketable farm produce as was being produced by the African population of seven or eight million.

Much of the farming by Africans then was done on very small plots. Much was intended not for the market, but for their own cooking pots. In some places the Kikuyu lived so closely packed, as close together as four hundred to the square mile, that it was all they could do to eke out an existence.

In the early days the white settlers had also had difficulties, enough to defeat the stoutest hearts. Little or nothing was known

about the climate, the rainfall, the qualities of the soil, about livestock diseases, about the pests and blights that attacked the crops.
Many early settlers lost all they had in learning the things that
would be of enormous benefit to those who followed. The trials
of Lord Delamere's first six years of farming were best summed
up in his own words:

"I had 3,000 acres under cultivation—mostly wheat—on the
Njoro farm alone, not counting Florida.

"The result after a few years of working was that sheep had
proved a failure and big losses had been incurred; that the land
had been proved unsuitable for improved cattle until the East
Coast fever menace was dealt with; that wheat was proved to
have come to stay. That the possibility of ploughing large acreages
in a country where the plough had never been seen was proved
to be an economic proposition; that large numbers of natives had
been taught ploughing and working with other implements; and
that I managed to get rid of £40,000 in cash which I had invested
in the country, and had for a time to live on about £200 a year
until a return began to materialize."

The white settlers—British, Scandinavians, Greeks, Italians,
Boers who trekked northward to Kenya from South Africa and
many others—went through a harsh process of trial and error, but
life for the African cultivator had always been a harsh, primitive
existence. He had always faced crop and livestock diseases, ticks
and tsetse fly and other insect pests, and periodic droughts. The
African farmer cleared a patch of bush by burning the trees and
scrub that covered it, and grew as much food as he needed to
sustain life in the family, often with little surplus for barter or for
storage against drought and crop failure in another year. Cattle
were kept as a sign of family wealth, and consumed only reluc-
tantly. After a few years, when the tsetse fly moved in, or when
the good soil was washed away or exhausted of its nutrients, the
African moved on to clear another patch of bush. He knew nothing of rotating or fertilizing crops; he simply broke new ground,
and left the old impoverished fields to retrieve their fertility by
lying fallow, or to deteriorate through erosion.

In this system of "shifting cultivation," there was no need for individual ownership of the land. The land within a tribal boundary was vested in the chief and he apportioned it to individuals for cultivation for as long as it would yield crops. The system was workable only as long as there was plenty of unoccupied land. It proved unsatisfactory in the more settled conditions that came with the white men's rule.

The arrival of Indians and white men in numbers was causing things to change. For the ambitious African, however, the way to change often seemed blocked by these alien races: the Indians had a grip on commerce and crafts; the white men held political power and the best agricultural land.

A feeling of nationalism bred easily in the gathering envy and resentment. The demand welled up for wider education, for equal treatment and, eventually, for political independence—*Uhuru*. From all this, Jomo Kenyatta rose as a symbol of African nationalism towering above all others.

He was called *Mzee*, the Swahili word for Old Man; the word was used with the great respect that accrues in African societies to the experience and wisdom that comes with age.

He did not know, any more than did most Africans of his generation, when he was born. An individual's age was of less significance to these people than was his age group, the whole group of village boys who were initiated together into manhood. The older ones in Jomo Kenyatta's age group were born about 1890.

His childhood home was a village called Mutoma; later the place came to be known as Ichaweri, in the Gatundu district. As a child he was not Jomo Kenyatta, but Kamau wa Ngengi. At mission school, he was christened Johnstone Kamau. As a young man in Nairobi, he took to wearing a beaded belt known as a *mucibi wa kenyatta,* the word *kenyatta* meaning "decorative" in Kikuyu. Soon he was being called Johnstone Kenyatta. During his stay in England later he dropped the Johnstone for Jomo, just because he liked the sound of it.

He had gone to Nairobi as a young man, attracted by the excitement of city life and driven by his ambition to do something about emancipating his people. He landed a job in 1921 as an inspector of water supplies. He began promoting the idea of independent schools for the Kikuyu, and was brushed almost immediately into the turmoil of politics.

By 1928, Kenyatta was general secretary of the Kikuyu Central Association, and was emerging as the real leader of the first nationalist movement in Kenya. A group of Indians put up money and legal help for Kenyatta so that he could plead the Kikuyu case for education and for social and political advancement with the colonial office in London. The Indians, with a larger community in Kenya than the British, calculated that if Kenyatta won some advantages for his own people, Indians were bound to benefit as well.

In London, Kenyatta fell in with the League Against Imperialism, a Communist group with its headquarters in that city. With the League's help, he visited Moscow and Berlin, and then went to Hamburg to attend the Communist-sponsored International Negro Workers' Congress. After eighteen months, Kenyatta's Indian backers lost patience with him and cut off his funds. He returned to Kenya in 1930, but only to go back to London again the next year.

This time he stayed away from his homeland for fifteen years, presenting petitions to the colonial office, writing letters to newspapers, ventilating African grievances in Trafalgar Square to anyone who would listen. In 1933 he spent four months in the Soviet Union, absorbing a little more about the tactics of revolution, meeting new friends. For a while, in London, he shared a flat near Charing Cross with Paul Robeson, the American singer and actor, and even appeared with him in a film version of Edgar Wallace's *Sanders of the River*. Kenyatta played the part of a native chief.

When World War II broke out, Kenyatta took a job as a farm laborer in Sussex, and was given the nickname "Jumbo" because of his bulk. He was remembered there as a good-natured man, given to reciting verses from Rudyard Kipling and to reading from Shakespeare's *Othello*.

On his return to Kenya in 1946 he led the demand for elected African representation in the legislative council. He wanted African voters on the electoral rolls. He wanted all manifestations of color discrimination abolished, and he wanted Africans back in the highland preserves of the white farmers.

But the colonial government was making no concessions, and while Kenyatta was talking of constitutional change, many of his followers were taking gruesome oaths to kill the white man, or terrify him into leaving the country.

By the middle of 1952, much of Kikuyu country had been swept up in the rebellion that came to be known as Mau Mau, and the great majority of the Kikuyu people either supported it actively or passively or were afraid to resist it. The Mau Mau gangs in the forests of the Aberdares and on Mount Kenya were well supplied with food and clothing, with stolen arms and ammunition, with women to tend for them. They had effective communication with Nairobi, by couriers, and were able to enforce a boycott of the buses, and of the smoking of cigarettes and the drinking of beer. The Mau Mau were able to raid and pillage over most of Kikuyuland and into the surrounding settled areas, for whoever was not a sympathizer was easily intimidated or killed.

Even the name of the movement had come to it through the secretive instincts of the Kikuyu and a word overheard, but misunderstood, by a British policeman in Naivasha.

The Kikuyu use a sort of Pig Latin to keep things to themselves, picking the first letter off a word and putting it in back. Thus, one night in 1948 when police were closing in on an oathing ceremony in Naivasha, one of the Kikuyu standing guard shouted *"Mau! Mau!"* and then everyone scattered in the darkness. The words meant nothing in themselves. *Mau* was an anagram for *Uma* which means "get away quickly." It was said twice for emphasis, as had been done with the name of the Maji Maji rebellion fifty years before in German East Africa.

The police never collected any convincing evidence linking Kenyatta with Mau Mau and not much against any of the real leaders of Mau Mau. But because no one among the Kikuyu could challenge the authority of Jomo Kenyatta, the British believed him to be responsible for Mau Mau, and decided to remove him from the scene.

In the predawn hours of October 20, 1952, the police, expect-

ing to surprise him in his sleep, found him fully dressed and
waiting stoically to be arrested. He was sentenced and imprisoned
at Lokitaung, a tiny police post in the barren northern desert,
close to the Sudan border.

The British then tried surrounding African settlements with
barbed wire and controlling the movements of people to and
from them, but the device did not stop the terror of Mau Mau.

In a sweep of Nairobi, called "Operation Anvil," many Kikuyu
were rounded up and detained. More such roundups were made
in Kiambu, Thika and Fort Hall, and then in Nyeri, Embu and
Meru. British planes bombed the Mau Mau gangs scattered on
Mount Kenya and in the Aberdares. By the end of 1954 mopping-
up operations were launched against them.

By the end of 1956, the rebellion was over. Only thirty-two
white civilians had been killed by Mau Mau. The toll of Africans
killed by Mau Mau was close to two thousand. The British had
lost sixty-three of the white men in their security forces. The Mau
Mau dead, by official British count, was put at 11,503.

Although Mau Mau had been broken as a military force, the
feeling for nationalism had not. The British accepted this, and
began preparing Kenya for independence.

After Kenyatta had served his seven-year prison sentence, he
was kept in detention and moved to Lodwar, still in the north.
From Lodwar he was moved eventually to Maralal, a mountain
oasis nearer Nairobi, then to Kiambu in his home district.

In August 1961, when he was finally released, Britain was
already speeding the transfer of power to her colony. Kenyatta
led his party to a sweep of the elections in May 1963, and was
asked by the British to form a transitional government, with himself as prime minister. On December 11, 1963, at the midnight
independence ceremony, Jomo Kenyatta shouted to a mass of
cheering people: "I have snatched you out of the lion's belly."

Afterward he never recalled the bitterness of the earlier days,
never tried to make political capital out of his long imprisonment.
He kept close ties with the British; to his way of thinking, it
would have been foolish and dangerous to dwell too long on past
iniquities, for other countries in Africa had done so and blinded

themselves to the hazards of political life in their own time.

Kenyatta had problems enough in confining the feelings of nationalism to the boundaries Kenya had inherited from the British. Many tribes disliked the boundaries, but none so adamantly as the Somali, the proud Hamitic people who roamed over the arid, empty frontier areas by the Somalia border. As far as the Somali were concerned, the border between Kenya and Somalia did not exist; they moved back and forth across it according to where the rain had fallen and where grass could be found for their camels and goats. They preferred to be independent, but if they had to join one country or another, they preferred to join Somalia, and to redraw the boundary to include the two-fifths of Kenya they claimed as theirs. They fought the Kenya army skillfully and hard for years to have their way, but eventually were defeated.

Arabs and Swahilis on the coast claimed autonomy for themselves in the ten-mile strip that had nominally belonged to the Sultan of Zanzibar. But the wealth and importance of the strip were derived from Mombasa, not from Zanzibar. A legal case could have been made for separate rule for the coastal strip, but as a practical matter it was dead.

Kenyatta would not allow his country to be nibbled away in the cause of separatism, nor his time and energy to be frittered away in histrionics about colonialism, imperialism, pan-Africanism or any other such things. His preoccupation was with practical matters.

As was the case with other former British territories, Kenya had become independent as one of Queen Elizabeth's dominions. The independence agreement had left executive authority vested formally in the queen, with a governor general in Kenya to exercise that authority for her. The fact that the authority was purely ceremonial did not make it go down any better with an old African nationalist who had spent his life removing all the vestiges of colonial rule. On the first anniversary of independence, Kenyatta proclaimed his country a republic, with executive authority vested openly in himself as president instead of indirectly in himself as Her Majesty's prime minister.

On most Monday afternoons, even as president, he would pull
up a chair in a square near his home and hear the criticisms and
suggestions of three or four hundred villagers who would gather
to talk to him. He would speak of unity and study the crowd, his
bleary, slow-moving eyes moving from one person to another. His
message was always a simple one: stop spending hard-earned
money on beer, stop idling, stop stealing; the British had been
toppled from power, but there was a new government and new
laws to be respected and obeyed; the fruits of independence
would not fall from trees, but had to be won by hard work.

This sort of talk never pleased the more radical politicians or
the more militant students. They grew impatient with Kenyatta,

*Jomo Kenyatta speaks at an Independence Day ceremony in Nairobi,
December 11, 1963. Behind him is the Mayor of Nairobi; seated at left,
H. R. H. The Duke of Edinburgh*

but could not challenge him. He always felt secure in taking the gradual approach. He felt it was the best way to keep the white settlers from leaving the big, productive farms too hurriedly, and to keep unprepared blacks from causing the farms to revert to patches of subsistence crops and bush. He did not want the public services to grind to a halt in a tangle of inefficiency. He did not want to frighten potential investors away, nor did he want any violent swings in politics to reopen the bitter tribal rivalries of an earlier age.

"*Harambee*," he always shouted at the end of his speeches. It is a Swahili chant the loggers use when they have to pull together. "*Harambee*," the crowds always shouted back.

Tanganyika had never been very militant about getting its independence, and had little need to be. After it ceased being a German colony after World War I, it became a League of Nations Mandate. After World War II it was made a United Nations Trust Territory. In both cases the British were left in administrative control. Because the trusteeship agreement stated that Britain was to prepare the country for independence, the people assumed they did not have to fight for it.

And yet, from the time it became clear that the British would be leaving, the Tanganyikans showed a latent rebelliousness, a resentment that whites and Indians were in positions of authority or were sitting on rich-looking farms. There was a clamor to have it all handed over to Africans, even though the unoccupied, uncultivated land in Tanganyika seemed almost endless.

By sheer will power and by his eloquence, Julius Kambarage Nyerere, then the prime minister of Tanganyika, later the president, and still later the president of Tanzania, carried his followers along a sophisticated, nonviolent path, although he had always been a radical in politics and a prolific generator of ideas. He was known to his people as *Mwalimu*—the Teacher.

Foreigners, too, were taken by the charm of this lissome, slight, cheerful man. He talked easily, and talked a lot. He loved to crack jokes, and then laugh at them heartily. He behaved much the same whether in front of an enormous crowd, or alone among friends in his gleaming palace overlooking the Indian Ocean.

He was born in 1922, the son of a Zanaki chief at Butiama on the Lake Victoria shore. Almost from the beginning it seemed Julius Nyerere had been cut out for a career as a teacher. After getting a diploma in education from Makerere College in Uganda, he taught at Tabora. After three years he entered Edinburgh University in Scotland to get a Master of Arts degree, and then resumed teaching, this time at Pugu, near Dar es Salaam.

But the demand for independence was blowing across Africa, and Nyerere drifted into politics. He helped organize the Tanganyika African Association, and was nominated by the British authorities to serve briefly on Tanganyika's legislative council.

When, in 1954, his association appeared to be submerging in a sea of competing political organizations, Nyerere led a drive to pull as many political factions as possible into a single national movement, the Tanganyika African National Union, and to make

*President Nyerere breaks ground for a housing project*

it serve as a single, powerful lever to hasten his country's independence.

Unity of a sort was easier to establish in Tanganyika than in Kenya or Uganda, for there were 128 tribes in the country, none powerful enough to dominate the others; because there were so many tribes, there never was a serious problem in politics of balancing one off against another, or of one advancing at the expense of all others.

Nyerere served again on the legislative council as a nominated member and then, after Tanganyika's first elections, in 1958, as an elected member. After the second elections, in 1960, Nyerere was asked to form a Council of Ministers. On independence he was sworn in as prime minister.

Six weeks later he resigned, but it was a political maneuver, one made necessary by the disappointment and lethargy that seemed to be settling over the people after they had got their independence.

Nyerere kept the chairmanship of the party to show that he meant to come back to power. Free of his government responsibilities, he toured villages in the most remote parts of the country, explaining to people that they would get nothing without working for it. Independence had been the single-minded goal, he explained, and having won it was only half the battle. The slogan of the country, he reminded them, was *"Uhuru na Kazi,"* the Swahili for "Freedom and Work."

Nyerere steered the offshore islands of Zanzibar and Pemba into the union with Tanganyika on April 22, 1964 that became known as Tanzania. To many people at the time it seemed a risky union for Tanganyika, for the islands' 270,000 Africans and Shirazis had taken power in a swift, brutal revolution against the Arab minority that had ruled Zanzibar. To many people on the mainland, the union raised the possibility that violence would be introduced to politics on the mainland and, because the Communist Chinese had become firmly entrenched in Zanzibar, that the island would be a base for subversion or a new form of imperialism.

There was no doubt that the revolution was a genuine one, and that support for it was widespread. Before the revolution, the land in Zanzibar had been held by forty-six families, mainly Arabs. They also held political power. After the revolution, only a third of the seventy-five thousand Arabs of Zanzibar and Pemba remained; the rest had fled in canoes and dhows to the mainland, or died in the fighting.

John Okello, the Ugandan who had appointed himself field marshal and led the islands' nine-hour revolution on January 11, 1964, claimed in his book, *Revolution in Zanzibar*, that 13,635 people were killed in the fighting and that only nine of them were members of his army of "furious soldiers."

Okello had moved to Zanzibar in 1959 at the age of twenty-one and worked on the sister island of Pemba for several years as a mason, painter and occasional laborer. As a mainland African he found a place for himself in the Afro-Shirazi Party, an African nationalist, anti-Arab union of blacks and people of mixed ancestry. By 1961 Okello was secretary of the party's youth wing on Pemba, plotting revolution.

When tension among the Africans and Shirazis rose after independence, the Sultan of Zanzibar betrayed his nervousness and his lack of political judgment by dismissing mainland Africans from his police force. Okello built the nucleus of his army around these disgruntled and jobless fighting men. Although Okello's account of the fighting was regarded in some ways as rather imaginative, some passages in his book suggest how the toll of Arab dead rose so high:

". . . I accompanied my men to round up forty-one Arab men who were hiding with eighteen women and ten children," he wrote. "I left them under guard to be collected by a lorry and taken to Zanzibar town for detention; but when the lorry arrived they had all been killed."

Those deaths he attributed to the fury of his soldiers, but Okello's wrath seemed easily aroused too, judging from his account of the ultimatum he issued to the sultan:

"You are allowed twenty minutes to kill your children and wives and then to kill yourself. I do not want to see your face and re-

*John Okello*

quest you to save me in this way from an unpleasant duty."

When he discovered that the sultan and most of his wives and attendants had already made their escape by yacht, Okello was furious.

"I became enraged," he wrote. "I ordered my soldiers to fire in all directions and to kill whatever came before them—men, women, children, disabled persons, even chickens and goats. Within a few seconds the destruction was enormous and flame soon consumed the huts and iron roofed buildings which were ignited with petrol."

As a Ugandan, Okello had no tribal power base on which to build a political career in Zanzibar. He had been paid a modest retainer by the Communist Chinese who wanted his favor, but he was edged off the island by the same Revolutionary Council he had appointed; the politicians took over from the self-made field marshal in the aftermath of revolution.

Abeid Amani Karume, a former seaman, established himself as President of Zanzibar through his leading position in the Afro-Shirazi Party and on the Revolutionary Council. While remaining President of Zanzibar, he also became First Vice-President of

Tanzania when the union with the mainland was brought into effect.

For as long as he could, Karume pursued an independent, somewhat erratic, ill-defined policy in Zanzibar and Pemba. He nationalized the land, but not the clove trees that grew on the land; the trees needed to be taken care of and only Arabs knew how. He issued a decree that the land would be turned into collective farms, but then he dropped the collectivization idea and began doling out three-acre parcels of land to families without any. To help the youngsters in the Afro-Shirazi Party youth wing raise money for the party, Karume gave them a monopoly to sell sugar, rice, salt, cigarettes and the most commonly bought items of food and clothing; the youngsters took over the stores, but had no idea about ordering things for the stores, or stocking them, and for a while there was chaos. The Revolutionary Council gave Karume the power to appoint a fourteen-member secret court to try political prisoners and pass sentences, including the death penalty, with no appeal except to Karume; but President Nyerere talked him out of appointing the court. Karume set up a system of forced labor, called *Kujitalea,* or "the voluntary rendering of one's services." He authorized the forced marriage of girls of Arab or Persian descent to members of the Revolutionary Council.

He described his policies as "Africanization with a vengeance." To keep his small, idle army from becoming a unified force strong enough to seize power, he put it into two camps, with one trained and equipped by the Chinese and the other by the Russians.

In Kenya, Okello drifted from bar to bar, slept in cheap hotels and squandered the small amounts of money the Chinese continued to give him. The Chinese bought him a new car in Kenya and Okello, who had never learned to drive, smashed it up almost immediately. The Chinese paid for the repairs, and Okello smashed the car up again. Then the Chinese dropped him.

Eventually he was banned from Kenya and Tanzania, and considered himself a worn and discarded tool of the politicians, or, as he wrote in his book: "the monkey who was allowed to clear the bush."

# CHAPTER 5

# THE RISE OF NATIONALISM:
# UGANDA

On the southern edge of Kampala, there is a broad avenue that leads up Mengo Hill between rows of giant candlenut trees and through a palisade of reeds to the old, imposing palace of the Kabaka of Buganda. In 1966, after the Uganda army stormed the palace and while the avenue was still blocked by one fallen candlenut tree and by the other debris of battle, President Apolo Milton Obote renamed it Republic Way. The Kabaka had escaped and he died in exile in London in 1969, but for years afterward the people around Mengo Hill continued to call the avenue by its old name: *Kabakanjagala*, meaning "The Kabaka Loves Me."

There were many signs of lingering affection for the Kabaka, Mutesa II, although there was little chance that the monarchy could ever be restored in anything like its old form. Even the Baganda had grown to accept that they would be governed as part of Uganda in a unified, republican state.

Of the forty or more ancient kingdoms that once were locked away in the heart of Africa from Lake Kyoga to Lake Tanganyika, four remained in Uganda in much their old form when Uganda got its independence from Britain in 1962. Besides the Kabaka of Buganda, there were the Omukama of Bunyoro, the Omugabe of Ankole, and the Omukama of Toro. The fifth monarch, the Kyabazinga of Busoga, was an elected one.

Obote's long campaign against the kingdoms contained within his country fits the pattern of revolutionary changes that were sweeping over East Africa after independence. These were complicated, many-sided revolutions, partly social and partly political, always a strain on the new national governments. Of the men who steered East Africa through its first formative years after independence, Obote faced the most intricate and explosive political problems.

The largest and most powerful of the kingdoms and the most pressing problem for Obote was Buganda, with two million of Uganda's eight million people. It spread over the capital and right around the fertile northwestern shore of Lake Victoria. It had its own police force, collected its own taxes, enacted its own laws. Its people had held a privileged position during the years of the British protectorate and the Baganda had wanted at the time of independence to be assured of a continued position of privilege and power; if they could not have that, they wanted to preserve a measure of autonomy, if not independence.

The awkward, overloaded Uganda government was also burdened with three recurring streams of refugees into the country: from Rwanda, the Congo and the southern Sudan. From time to time the wars in the Congo and in the southern Sudan spilled across the borders into Uganda. On both borders, there were tribes that straddled the political frontier, treating the frontier as though it did not exist.

Even within Uganda a rebellion had simmered for years among the Bakonjo and the Bwamba in the Ruwenzori Mountains. There had been a running tribal war between the Sebei and the Bagisu on Mount Elgon, another between the Karamojong and the Sebei, intermittent battles between factions of the Karamojong and constant harassment from cattle-rustling tribes on the Kenya border.

Not many people gave Obote a chance to survive that political jungle. Through his hazardous political career his contemporaries

*Mutesa II, Kabaka of Buganda,*
*at his birthday celebration in 1951*

were repeatedly surprised by his staying power, and by his skill and agility as a politician.

He had been a dark horse, and a late starter. Even his father, a minor Lango chief, waited until Milton Obote was twelve before deciding finally that it was worth the expense to send him to school, as he had the other children.

Milton Obote was born in 1924 in Akakoror, a village on Lake Kwania. Because he started so late in school, he spent more years than did most of Africa's rulers tending his father's cattle and goats.

He was dropped from high school a couple of times because of his grades. He withdrew from Makerere College after two years. The British colonial authorities discouraged him from going to the United States or to the Sudan to study, because of his poor academic record and his indecisiveness.

He studied by correspondence, and drifted to Nairobi, looking for work or adventure wherever he could find it. He heaved sacks of sugar, worked for an oil company as a clerk, finally got involved in trade unionism and in street politics and found he liked it.

In 1957, after eight years, he returned to Uganda and became active in the strife-ridden Uganda National Congress. He pulled a group away from the party and formed the Uganda People's Congress in 1960, with himself as president of the new party.

By good fortune, Obote was leader of Uganda's parliamentary opposition when Buganda decided to boycott parliament, to press its demand for secession from Uganda and independence on its own. It was an unpopular move outside Buganda, and Obote led his party to a fairly easy win in the elections before independence.

His party was the largest in parliament then, but still did not have a majority. When Buganda politicians started having second thoughts about the wisdom of their threats to secede and their boycott, Obote forged an unnatural and uneasy coalition with them, and the balance of power tipped to his side.

Obote had no real choice in the negotiations that led to independence but to make a compromise with the rich old kingdom. It was allowed to continue to enact laws and to enforce them, and to collect taxes. The Baganda members of Uganda's parliament were not popularly elected as were other members, but were selected by Buganda's own parliament, the Lukiiko, acting as an electoral college.

Obote became the prime minister of independent Uganda and the Kabaka was accepted as the constitutional president, not as Kabaka Mutesa II, but as an individual: Sir Edward Frederick Walugembe Mutesa.

Eventually, instead of a movement to secede, there was a steady movement into Obote's party, the Uganda People's Congress. Most of the Baganda and other Bantu people who joined the party then favored a strong unified republic, but they also wanted to see power shifted from non-Bantu northerners like Obote to the more numerous Bantu people spread across the southern half of the country.

When five of his Bantu ministers pressed him on February 22,

1966, to set a date for elections, Obote had them dragged by police out of the cabinet meeting and put in detention. The army commander, Brigadier Shabani Opoloto, was put in detention when Obote began to suspect his loyalty, as were hundreds of others— magistrates, members of parliament, tribal chiefs, civil servants, newspaper editors and reporters.

Obote took over all powers of government on the night of February 22, 1966, and on April 16 introduced a temporary new constitution that wiped out what powers the kingdoms still had. The constitution was accepted unread by parliament by a show of hands of forty-five to five, with thirty-three members abstaining. It was a curious sight, as parliament had also ceased formally to exist. Obote addressed the members as "fellow citizens" and asked them, in effect, to accept the end of their existence. With soldiers in the gallery, armed with automatic rifles and peering down at them, the legislators had little choice.

On the same day, Obote proclaimed Uganda a unified republic

*Milton Obote in 1965*

and was sworn in as president. Sir Edward Mutesa, who had been deprived of power both as Kabaka of Buganda and President of Uganda, appealed to the United Nations to intervene. When it did not, the Kabaka's legislature ordered the Uganda government out of the Kingdom of Buganda; in other words, as both Buganda and Uganda had their capital in the same city, the Uganda government was being ordered out of its capital. The eviction notice was an act of rebellion, well understood by the Baganda, for the sound of war drums began rolling down from the hills around town and the Baganda gathered with crude weapons around the Kabaka, waiting for the attack.

On May 24, 1966, at dawn, the army did attack. Three days later the battle was over. Perhaps two thousand Baganda had died in the fighting, although the army kept the Red Cross and Ministry of Health workers from removing the dead or tending the wounded, and establishing the real extent of the casualties. One obvious casualty had been the frail concept of orderly and constitutional rule in Uganda.

Obote accepted this reproof, or at least listened to it. Before he closed down a lively, outspoken magazine called *Transition* and detained its editor, Rajat Neogy, President Obote had even contributed his views to the publication, including his contention that Uganda was not ready for real parliamentary democracy; Uganda ought to have it eventually, he said, but to get it prematurely would plunge the country into the pattern of upheaval and trial and error suffered by every country where parliamentary democracy had been achieved.

He did not contend the trouble in Uganda would come from ordinary people. Obote blamed the wealthier, better educated elite for the bulk of his problems; he worried about the army, and about the ambitious politicians around him, especially after he was shot in the jaw in an assassination attempt in 1969.

On January 25, 1971, when he was returning to Uganda from a Commonwealth conference in Singapore, Obote was deposed by his army commander, Major General Idi Amin, a powerfully built former heavyweight boxing champion of Uganda, a man who had risen through the ranks, and who had seen service with the King's

African Rifles in Burma during World War II, and in Kenya during the Mau Mau crisis.

General Amin claimed that the army's takeover had been defensive, that it had been done only to forestall a plan by Obote to remove him from the head of the army, and possibly to kill him. General Amin's predecessor had been imprisoned. Two of the general's subordinates died in suspicious circumstances.

Obote had begun to distrust Amin a year before; although the general was from the West Nile District, in the far northwestern part of the country, he had been making friends with a group of Baganda Moslems who Obote felt were working against him. Obote began to bypass Amin in military matters and then, in September, reorganized the command structure of the armed services in a way that sharply reduced Amin's power.

On the night before the coup a small group of officers loyal to Obote directed that an armory be seized, and Amin arrested. Their plan was discovered by Amin's better organized forces before they could carry it out. Some scattered fighting lasted about twelve hours. About a hundred people were killed. A dozen officers behind the move against Amin were summarily executed and others were arrested.

Obote did not attempt at first to get back to Uganda. He tried to issue a statement from Nairobi, but was prevented from doing so by President Kenyatta. Obote moved on to Dar es Salaam where President Nyerere allowed him to speak as critically of General Amin as he wanted.

In his years in power, Obote had been obsessed with his vision of hammering all the old feudal and tribal parts of Uganda into a single nation. His aim had been national unity, but he moved so fast that cracks kept appearing in the facade of unity. A national consciousness was being developed while politics was still bound up intimately with tribal allegiances. Buganda's threatened secession had come to nothing, but it emphasized the intensity of feeling among the Baganda that never subsided in Obote's time.

Trade unions, education, new religious sects, new political organizations and alliances and many other factors were slowly changing things, but peace and the promised good life still proved

*Major General Idi Amin drives through crowds after deposing President Obote in January, 1971*

elusive. In many ways the ordinary man's life was still governed too much by poverty, ignorance and disease, still too bound up in the old tribal ways.

Obote was a moody person; he could be extremely cordial or he could burst out suddenly in fury and rage. He gathered enormous power in his own hands, yet he did not live ostentatiously. He picked at his food. He smoked constantly. Sometimes he would talk for hours about politics if he thought the persons listening were really interested.

In 1969 he had announced a "move to the left" to his people, but few of the people who knew him thought it was anything more than a political device, a tactic for some reason of internal politics. Obote had political vision, but he never encouraged people around him to think he had an ideology.

"I have none, except pragmatism," he once said.

# CHAPTER 6

# AFRICAN SOCIALISM

In April 1966 two dissident members of parliament from the north
of Kenya marched in the company of a dozen tribal elders to State
House in Nairobi to see President Kenyatta. To hear the men in
this colorful little group speak, no outsider would have suspected
that any of them had in any way been unfaithful to *Mzee,* or that
these same two members of parliament had, a few days before,
followed Jaramogi Oginga Odinga into the new opposition party,
the Kenya People's Union.

"We cannot listen to those who say the government has done
nothing since independence, while around us we witness changes
taking place every day in the development of the country," one
of the elders said. "This is a thing we could not see before we
gained independence through your indisputable leadership."

The president embraced the two members as though they had
never left the ranks of the Kenya African National Union, and
said it was only the blind ones who were going their own way.
With this reconciliation the incipient political revolution was
stopped before it really got started. More dissidents returned to

Kenyatta's fold and within a few days Odinga's new party was a spent force.

That there should be no formal opposition was in keeping with Kenyatta's version of "African Socialism." On April 27, 1965, he told the Kenya parliament that African Socialism was an ideology apart from both capitalism and communism, one that would combine political democracy with social responsibility and draw for its inspiration on African traditions.

It promised that various forms of ownership would continue to be accepted and encouraged in Kenya, and that state ownership or joint ventures between state and private investors would be tried when it seemed right, and when the government's resources and other needs permitted it to undertake such ventures.

"African Socialism differs politically from communism because it ensures every mature citizen equal political rights, and from capitalism because it prevents the exercise of disproportionate political influence by economic power groups," Kenyatta said.

This did not mean that the brand of radicalism Odinga represented would disappear from the political scene. There was a real clamor for land that white men still farmed in the highlands, for jobs in the civil service that white men still held, for free universal education. Many Kenyans never got over their disappointment that independence did not in itself throw open the gates on a great, golden age of radical economic change in which Africans would sit at the levers of wealth and power.

Because of the popular demand for Africanization, the more radical politicians in East Africa faced a real dilemma: if they wanted radical economic change, they could hardly advocate that Africans take over the jobs and farms of the white elite, or the shops of the Indian *duka-wallahs*. To Africanize the existing system would have been to keep it intact, but in the hands of black capitalists instead of brown or white ones.

Speaking to the graduating class at Makerere University College in Kampala in 1965, Kenyatta tried to explain the apparent paradox, and to put across his view that to impose communism or some other imported form of revolutionary change would be futile:

"It is quite fundamental that economic development must reflect and be built around the life of the people. Alien and unwanted systems cannot and will not last.

"We have not yet found all the answers. *Uhuru* opens up a whole new universe, composed of those reactions and ambitions that for so long were locked away in people's minds."

To enfold the whole of political life within a single party organization was a device tried in all three East African countries. It reflected the communal nature of traditional African society. It carried the built-in risk of the more powerful tribes seeking to rule the others, but it was far more acceptable to the East Africans than were the parliamentary systems they had inherited from Britain.

Traditionally, when decisions needed to be made by Africans, everyone in the village gathered for a *baraza*—a long, long talk. Sometimes these sessions went on for days, restarting each morning in the shade of a spreading thorn tree. The men talked about the vagaries of the weather, the problems of wives and children and troublesome neighboring tribes and anything else that came to mind.

There was no open argument. The speeches were punctuated with general sounds of approval or disapproval from the other men, or from the women and children who sat at the edges of the crowd, but no votes were taken. No one openly conceded a point. When everyone had his say, the *baraza* was over. By this time everyone had agreed, or been persuaded that there was no point in continuing the discussion.

Just as it was difficult for these people to grasp the concept of a formal opposition, so was it difficult to explain to them why all three East African governments had accepted with independence a formal tie to the British Crown. In fact, all had accepted the tie as a compromise to hasten independence, and all three broke the tie soon afterward. For the people, their own national leaders symbolized independence and unity, not a powerless queen in London. This was true even of those who were against unity or who feared they would see their tribal identity or their personal ambitions submerged in it.

That Kenyatta was accepted as a symbol of unity in Kenya was evident from the array of spears and shields and other traditional tokens of submission that were given to him by tribal chiefs.

In the first year of independence Ronald Ngala, the opposition leader, announced that his dwindling party, the Kenya African Democratic Union, had dissolved itself and was joining Kenyatta's party in the interests of national unity.

In 1969, after Tom Mboya, the Minister of Economic Planning and Development, was assassinated in a Nairobi street and members of Mboya's Luo tribe began rioting, the president blamed Oginga Odinga for stirring up tribal tensions. Kenyatta detained Odinga and nineteen of his colleagues in the Kenya People's Union for seventeen months, effectively making Kenya a one-party state again. A few months after independence Kenyatta had said a one-party state was his aim:

"We reject a blueprint of the western model of a two-party system of government because we do not subscribe to the notion of the government and the governed in opposition to one another, one clamoring for duties and the other crying for rights."

Nyerere's brand of socialism was different. He hoped to fire popular imagination with schemes for self-help and community effort, and called his ideology *ujamaa*. This is the Swahili word for "family," and suggests the social responsibility that revolves around the family.

For some Tanzanians, only the name was new. The Wapare people below Kilimanjaro know the system as *msaragambo*, although it is the same. The roads leading through Mwanza, Usangi and Ugweno, with a total length of more than two hundred miles, were built over a period of forty years to connect the nine chiefdoms of Pare. The men, women and children of the tribe who built the roads were summoned regularly to continue the work long after independence.

The pre-independence slogan of Freedom and Work got translated into such community self-help schemes around the country with varying degrees of success, and into regulations that land had to be used or given up. In October 1966 the work ethic was transformed into National Service, a two-year period of service to the state on road construction, irrigation projects and such.

When the students at the University College in Dar es Salaam learned that it would apply to them on graduation, that they could work in their professions but get only a minimum wage and pay the rest of their salaries for that time into National Service funds, they simmered for a week and then decided to demonstrate. Chanting and carrying placards, 393 of them marched on

the office of the Second Vice-President, Rashidi Kawawa, the man responsible for administering National Service.

Armed, steel-helmeted riot police diverted the march to State House where President Nyerere and fifteen cabinet ministers were waiting for them. The president was smiling and seemed to be in a jovial mood. If the students had seen a letter Nyerere had written from Scotland to Makerere College in the days when he was a student, they might have been more skeptical:

*President Kenyatta (second from right)*
*accepts a spear from a tribal elder.*
*At far right is Tom Mboya*

"While I was at Makerere I understood that my government was spending something in the neighborhood of £80 on my behalf . . . " he wrote then. "I wonder whether it has ever occurred to many of us that while that £80 was being spent on me (or for that matter on any other of the past or present students of Makerere) some village dispensary was not being built in my village or some other village. People may actually have died through lack of medicine merely because eighty pounds which could have been spent on a fine village dispensary were spent on me, a mere individual, instead . . . "

"Why did the community spend all that money, run all those risks . . . ? " Nyerere asked rhetorically in the letter. "Was it for the sake of building a magnificent but useless apex of a stagnant pyramid? Surely not. The community spends all that money upon us because it wants us as lifting levers, and as such we must remain low and bear the whole weight of the masses to be lifted, and we must facilitate that task of lifting."

Nyerere listened to the complaints of the students who sat before him on the grass at State House. They argued that they would be made to suffer financially by National Service, while high government officials did not think of making sacrifices themselves. The students did not need the training in discipline as did the uneducated people in the country, the students argued. They could be made to join National Service in body but not in spirit, they said.

Nyerere applauded when the students had finished talking. He had thought long about the problem, he said, and had decided that the students should be taken into National Service only after graduation, so that their studies would not be interrupted.

The students were right to complain about the need for high government officials to make sacrifices, Nyerere said. He announced that he was cutting his own salary by 20 percent, not for two years, but permanently. Other officials would suffer salary cuts, the president told the flabbergasted students. The smile had gone from his face, and the anger was showing.

"You and I are the same class, the exploiting class," he said.

"Go home," he told the students. It took them a few days to discover that they had been expelled from the university, and forbidden to hold paying jobs for two years. Five months later Nyerere relented and let the students take jobs, and held out the hope that most of them might eventually be able to resume their studies.

Still, his stern treatment of the students was enormously popular with people around the country who envied the students for having got so far in their education, and who resented them as a privileged and elite group. Demonstrations against the students spread to the most remote villages, and to Zanzibar, and paved the way for the austere form of socialism Nyerere announced in Arusha in February 1967.

After that public commitment to socialism and self-reliance, known as the Arusha Declaration, the banks were nationalized. Within two days the nationalization had been widened to include mills and factories, import and export houses, insurance companies and other big businesses and plantations in Tanzania. The declaration was named for the town in which it was proclaimed. It became Tanzania's basic policy document, providing the guidelines for future edicts and legislation, and announcing the end of special privileges and of Tanzania's heavy dependence on outside help and cooperation, even from her neighbors in East Africa.

Nyerere had already shaken the East African Community a year before when he had introduced a separate currency and separate monetary controls for Tanzania. Until that time, Kenya, Uganda and Tanzania, the three members of the organization, had used a common currency as they had in British days.

Now his new actions threatened the Community's common market and the many services that the three countries shared, such as the railroads and harbors, the airline, the postal services, customs and excise and income tax collection, telephone and other communications, the university and research facilities and a court of appeal.

Nationalization also shook the confidence of foreign investors in Tanzania, but foreign investment had never been adequate.

"The Arusha Declaration did not cause miracles," Nyerere explained to his party later that year. "It did not make the crops more fruitful or the rains more regular. It did not make everyone wealthy, nor change the level of our education.

"We have no more become a socialist country because of the Arusha Declaration than a young boy becomes a good Christian or a good Moslem by the act of dedication. The sincere act of dedication is important, but much more important are the actions which follow during his life."

Nyerere insisted that the party must be more than an electoral, policy-making machine. Each of its officers had to consider himself a worker or peasant, and take responsibility for explaining policy throughout the country. The party leaders were forbidden to hold shares in private companies, or to be directors of any. No leader could receive more than one salary, or own a house that he rented to others.

Some Tanzanian leaders put their houses in the names of their wives or children, and disguised their directorships in private companies. But evasion was difficult for the politicians, for the Arusha Declaration was popular with the people.

Most popular of all was the rule that the party leaders had to drive moderately priced cars instead of the big limousines that had led the people to call them the Wabenzi—the tribe of the Mercedes-Benz.

Tanzania had been the first of the East African countries to create a one-party state by law. Nyerere realized the dangers of a monolithic ruling party, however. He knew the risks of smothering criticism and constructive argument and political ambition.

His solution was a new version of the single-party state. His own position was not challenged through this special electoral process, but in every other district in Tanzania there were two candidates to choose from, even though both were members of the same party.

At the first such one-party election, in September 1965, two of Nyerere's cabinet ministers lost their elections and their seats in

*Kenyatta, waving, with Nyerere (left) and Obote*
*at an East African conference in 1964*

parliament. At the election in 1970, two more cabinet ministers were defeated.

In Uganda, Obote's interest in African Socialism as an ideology came late in his political career; even then he showed little enthusiasm over it. In the last year before he was deposed, he made efforts to swing Uganda toward socialism with a "Common Man's Charter." In May 1970, he began negotiations with banks and insurance companies about the government buying an interest in them, perhaps a controlling interest, but the negotiations came to nothing.

He stated his preference for a one-party system on several occasions. For years he worked to achieve his aim by patronage and persuasion. He had the green and white traffic signs in Kampala repainted, because these were the colors of the Democratic Party, the last opposition party.

He finally banned all opposition after he was shot in the jaw in an assassination attempt on December 19, 1969, as he left Lugogo Stadium Hall in Kampala in a stream of people, after closing a conference of the Uganda People's Congress.

The man who deposed him, General Idi Amin, went much further with a decree on March 23, 1971, that imposed a two-year ban on all processions, proclamations, pamphlets, meetings, flags and uniforms and anything else that could be associated with political activity.

While Obote was still in power he seemed to thrive on criticism and very often heeded it, at least to a limited extent. After his army had overrun Mengo Hill in 1966 and shattered the last resistance that had mustered around the Kabaka, Obote had introduced a temporary republican constitution abolishing the kingdoms, consolidating his own power, and making other reforms.

When he introduced a permanent new constitution in 1967, the constitutional debate lasted for three months. With a majority in Parliament then of sixty-three to nine, Obote did not have to worry about the outcome of the debate, but he was in the thick of it the whole time. He permitted some of his personal powers to be trimmed marginally. He said afterward that without the stimulation of criticism and debate he would have been a poorer president.

The Uganda People's Congress was still committed to the idea of a voluntary one-party state, although some party leaders were full of doubts about how they should control the divergent political interests that would be locked together in a single party.

There was some support within the party for perpetuating it by making Uganda a non-party state, by transforming the Uganda People's Congress into a "Congress of the People" that could not be challenged.

All this was too utopian for President Obote, who had to cope with realities in his career, including opposition that was inspired by tribal or religious or personal differences.

One of his great problems, he felt, was that the colonial experience had left ordinary people in Uganda with a deep, abiding resentment of authority.

An overriding problem, he wrote, stemmed from the autocratic tradition of the Kabaka and his court, and from people who, because of wealth or race, supported the Kabaka's demand for special constitutional safeguards, expecting that they would profit by the safeguards, too.

"These attitudes meant that the ordinary man is incapable of ruling or influencing government policy," Obote wrote in 1968. "The corollary of this is that the offspring of chiefs, landowners and people associated with the court, were the only people qualified for leadership. In short, the criterion was, in Luganda, *Mwana wani?* (Whose child?) . . .

"This situation contributed greatly to the revolution of 1966 when there was a confrontation between democracy and autocracy."

# CHAPTER 7

# AFRICAN REALITY

"It was not the masses who caused chaos," President Milton Obote said in 1967 in the Constitutional Assembly, as Uganda's National Assembly was called when it was reconstituted for the long debate on the new republican constitution. "It was not the masses who had brought shame on Africa. It was those who sat in the parliaments of Africa and those who saw the inside of universities and those who had seen the light of modern society. These were the people who had given Africa her present shape. It was such people as these who would not hesitate to see that an African state was plunged into difficulties in the hope that these difficulties would provide them with personal advantages."

Obote was suspicious of the elite and was inclined to play up to the masses this way. Yet the masses were causing chaos in many places in East Africa, sometimes by clinging too long to their old ways, sometimes by plunging headlong into new ways.

In Mombasa, for example, thousands of families from villages close to the coast settled on the edge of town in a place they called California, eking out an existence in hovels made of pack-

ing crates and cardboard. Many of them made their living by
carving wooden figures for tourists; there was almost no other
prospect of work for them.

There were squatters' villages like this in all the big towns in
East Africa, many of them holding thousands of people who
worked in the town or looked for work there. They drew their
water from muddy streams, or from shallow, polluted wells. The
fact that these people had no title to the land on which they
were squatting bothered the authorities less than the squalor and
the fear that cholera or plague or some other disease would
spread uncontrollably. Many of the squatters' villages were
burned down by the police and health authorities regularly, but
they went right up again.

In the highlands of Kenya and northern Tanzania, Africans
moved from their villages to the edges of the big farms of white
men and of the big settlement schemes of the governments. Often
they farmed little patches of land by the fences. Often they were
encouraged by local politicians to stay where they were if they
wanted more land.

Their disappointment at not getting more land gave rise to
much hard feeling, and often to theft of a sort not customarily
known in East Africa. Often, when they were hungry or angry,
the squatters would knock a fence down and clean out a field of
every last ear of corn, and then defy the owners or the authorities to do something about it. In other cases, theft had been an
honorable and long-established custom.

For years after independence, on every moonlit night, on the
fringes of Masailand and Karamoja and over vast tracts of grazing
land in East Africa, hundreds of cattle were driven by thieves
from their *bomas,* the thorn fence enclosures where they belonged,
to *bomas* where they did not belong, or to makeshift slaughterhouses in the bush. The police became faster and more efficient,
and returned many of the rustled cattle, although often in such
poor condition that they had to be destroyed.

In Uganda, the Karamojong and the Sebei were constantly
sending raiding parties after each other's cattle. Sometimes they
carried their raids across the Kenya border against the Turkana,

*A slum dwelling in Nairobi, Kenya*

or the Suk, who sometimes carried out raids across the border themselves. In Kenya there was constant battle between the Turkana, the Rendille, the Boran and the Suk.

But the most notorious of all were the Masai, whose warriors had nothing to do but preen their bodies with ocher and their hair with ocher and fancy braids, and to prove themselves before their peers and the young women of the tribe.

In the years when Kenya and Tanganyika were under British rule, the Masai were discouraged from battling with neighboring tribes, killing men and stealing women. With this predatory function more or less gone, the warriors were left with only lion fighting and cattle rustling as means by which they could establish their reputations.

The white settlers had learned to live with the thieving, partly out of respect for the mysterious devotion the Masai have to cattle and the kinship they feel for these animals, but mainly because the Masai always admitted to the thefts when they were caught, and accepted their fines or penalties with dignity and a certain amount of pride. The Masai have a tradition that all the cattle in the world belong to them; when they seem to be stealing cattle, they are merely repatriating them, that is, bringing them back to the tribe.

But as African farmers began setting up larger farms, or banding together in settlement schemes, they took less kindly to cattle thieving. An African farmer trying to get established with a herd of half a dozen head of cattle could be ruined in a night by a small band of rustlers; he could easily lose his life by resisting.

Early in 1967, President Nyerere bid the public help police round up suspected cattle thieves in Tanzania. More than four thousand Masai and Wakuria and others from tribes where cattle rustling had been an honorable tradition were rounded up, along with some others from tribes where no such tradition existed. Also, many of the rounded-up men were too old to be rustlers, and had been found window-shopping or otherwise lingering in Arusha. Nyerere asked the public to be patient, to give the police a chance to screen out the innocent ones.

But the Tanzanian farmers were angry. A year later, when nine suspects were caught in Sungwizi village, they were not handed over to the police; they were lynched.

In the towns, too, there was a feeling of outrage over the rising incidence of crime and violence after independence. Burglars and housebreakers had rarely been armed before. Most common of all had been the "polefishers," thieves who poked fishing poles through the barred but open windows on homes, fishing for clothes, blankets, radios and anything else within reach that was not too heavy to be reeled in.

Violence in the towns had usually begun when a crowd caught

up with a thief. Unless the police arrived in time to rescue him, the crowd trampled and beat him to death, even if he had stolen nothing more than a trinket or a ten-shilling note.

In Uganda the Kondo gangs, named from an old Swahili word for violence, increasingly raided isolated African homes, often killing or maiming their victims. So numerous were the gangs and so terrified the population, that on June 20, 1968, the Uganda parliament made it mandatory for a judge to impose the death penalty on convicted thieves who used or threatened to use deadly weapons in the course of a robbery, and for anyone who took part in the robbery, armed or not.

This stiffened penalty may have had an exciting effect on the population of Uganda, for three months later a mob intercepted a policeman and a tribal chief escorting seven alleged thieves to police headquarters at Gombola. Four of the men, handcuffed together, were beaten to death on the spot. A fifth was caught on the run and killed. The villagers then launched a manhunt in the bush to find and kill the other two. Even the chief and the policeman were beaten severely for trying to protect the arrested men.

In Zanzibar the courts were deprived of most of their old authority. After July 1968, only cases of murder and armed robbery could be tried in courts. All other criminals or suspected criminals were sentenced automatically to five years in prison. Political offenders on that revolutionary island were treated even more harshly, as was enunciated by President Karume:

"Any leader found to be leaning toward capitalist ideology or practicing capitalism itself will render himself liable to imprisonment until his or her natural death."

One of the biggest hindrances to the attempts that were made in East Africa to maintain an orderly legal procedure was the resurgence of tribalism. It burst to the surface in Kenya after the assassination of Tom Mboya on July 5, 1969. He had been the Minister for Economic Planning and Development, one of the brightest and most promising members of Kenyatta's government.

Mboya had made a deliberate effort through his career to rise

*Mboya campaigning for election in 1961*

above tribal politics. He was a Luo, a member of Kenya's second
biggest tribe, but he was elected to parliament from a Nairobi
constituency, not from the Luo country around Lake Victoria.
Yet when he was gunned down as he came out of a Nairobi drug-
store, the Luos went on a rampage, rioting in Nairobi and all
around Kisumu in Luo country. When Kenyatta's blue Mercedes
limousine arrived in Luo country for a memorial service for Tom
Mboya, it was stoned.

Kenyatta had never been so seriously challenged before, and

the idea of the people of his own tribe, the Kikuyu, swearing their loyalty in oaths was put to the president.

The ritual oath taking began at the president's farm at Icha-weri, with men and women swearing in weird rites that the Kenya flag would never leave the house of Numbi, the wife of Gikuyu, the mythical founder of the tribe. The oath taking spread through Kikuyuland, much like the oath taking that had made Mau Mau so fearsome and powerful. But as long as the Kikuyu leadership in Kenya was unchallenged there was no violence from the Kikuyu and no need for it.

In Tanzania, the revolutionary fervor had little to do with tribalism; it was attributed to unavoidable and natural circumstances. Independence had come at the end of a year that showed no increase in national income. The production of sisal fiber used in the manufacture of rope and matting had slumped. Competition from synthetic fibers was being felt. A drop in world prices hit the sisal growers and they laid off some of their workers. Low world prices hit the coffee growers the same way and the situation continued to worsen in the years that followed.

The confusion, disappointment and resentment that built up around Tanzania found an outlet in outbursts against the other, better-off races. White men's farms were confiscated in Tanzania. Indian charcoal sellers and barbers were thrown out of their shops in Dar es Salaam. Soon, the ones who still held British or Indian passports were being deported. In Kenya and Uganda the politicians quickly took to the idea of making the Indians their targets for abuse.

These were the families who had come, or whose forebears had come, to Africa to escape the distressing poverty of the Indian subcontinent. The first began to arrive as traders, centuries before, borne across the Indian Ocean on the monsoon winds. By far the greatest influx, however, arrived toward the end of the nineteenth century, when the British imported thirty thousand Indians to build the railroad and the complex of shops and facilities along it. So extensive was Indian influence in those days that the Indian rupee was the official coinage, and the Indian

laws for marriage, divorce, inheritance and many other religious
and personal matters were applied in East Africa.

By independence, there were four hundred thousand Indians
living and trading among thirty million Africans in the three
countries. Yet they controlled probably four-fifths of the commerce, from the biggest trading houses to the smallest *duka* in
the bush.

The Indians' religious, traditional and social divisions made
them as different from one another as possible—Goan Christians,
Ismaili Moslems, Sikhs with their beards tucked up into their
*puggrees.* A few of the women had taken to modern European
dress, but most stuck to their banian ways, or to fashionable new
versions of their traditional dress: the form-hugging *khamis* and
*salwar* of the Moslem women, the bright saris wrapped in misty
folds around the gliding, dusky figures of the Hindu women.

To Africans, however, these people all seemed pretty much

*Asians shop at an Indian store in Mombasa*

alike—remote, rather mysterious. In the evenings and on Sundays, whole families streamed out of their blocks of shops and flats to promenade, walking in slightly separated groups. With their obvious wealth and strange ways and their ties to communities far away, the Indians remained a world apart from the Africans, and became more and more the objects of outbursts of envy and resentment.

"Bloodsuckers," shouted Joseph Nyerere at a rally when he was regional commissioner in Mwanza, on the shore of Lake Victoria. Joseph Nyerere, the president's brother, told a crowd that an Indian mill owner had bought diamonds and taken them out to India. Mr. Nyerere asked the crowd what ought to be done to the man.

"Kill him!" the crowd demanded. Such men deserved hanging, the commissioner agreed, but this one had already been deported. Only the mill was still in Tanzania.

"Confiscate it!" the crowd yelled. This, too, had already been done; the mill had been turned over to the party's youth league.

Anti-Indian outbursts like that were common in East Africa. They betrayed frustrations stemming from the fact that while the Africans had won political independence, economic power still eluded them. Programs of government help to aspiring African businessmen had not often proved as useful in the hard world of business as hard work and the business sense that is acquired through experience, and the credit and contacts an Indian could find more easily than could an African.

Too few Indians had given up their Indian or British passports to suit the Africans, who resented the divided loyalty, the foot in the door between two worlds, the apparent desire to have the best of both and the obligations of neither. To the ambitious African, the Indian was also the man on the next rung up on the ladder; for that reason it was popular and politically necessary for the East African leaders to remove Indians from certain jobs or from certain areas.

When the numbers of deportees rose steeply, Britain introduced legislation to bar the entry of Indians with British passports, except within a narrow quota. But that was a British problem, not an East African one, and from Kenya, Uganda and Tanzania the Indians were sent in large numbers, and hoped for the best. In Zanzibar, the Indians had been divested of all they had soon after the revolution, and most had left.

Many of those who left were skilled men, artisans who could not easily be replaced, or *duka-wallahs* who operated on such small margins of profit that no one was attracted to their businesses.

Their departure may have opened new possibilities for Africans in the long run to get control over their own economies. In the short run, however, the departure of the Indians and the whites was of doubtful economic usefulness. The level of wealth in East Africa was so small and the untrained, underemployed labor force was increasing so rapidly that each time a mechanic or plumber or potential employer was removed, it was as likely to hurt East Africa as it was to help.

Each such unrewarding move left the Africans feeling all the more deeply that they could not by themselves make things change for the better. It was this feeling to which Chou En-lai, Premier of the People's Republic of China, alluded on June 5, 1965, when he addressed a mass rally in the National Stadium in Dar es Salaam, at the start of a visit to Tanzania.

"An exceedingly favorable situation for revolution prevails today, not only in Africa, but also in Asia and Latin America," the Chinese premier said.

# CHAPTER 8

# THE BUBBLING CALDRON

In July 1970, clouds of choking white dust billowed upward from a swarm of bulldozers and trucks and other earth-moving machines on the dry plain on the edge of Dar es Salaam. Communist Chinese engineers and drivers worked relentlessly in the moist heat, scraping up the chalky dirt, shifting it and pounding it into a roadbed for the railroad that was to reach from that sleepy, picturesque Tanzanian port to Kapiri Mposhi, more than a thousand miles away, near the rich copper mines of Zambia.

For years the railroad project had been discouraged by officials and experts from the United States, Britain and elsewhere as unnecessary and uneconomic, or inadequately considered, or unwise because of the many other needs in Tanzania and Zambia for funds. To the Africans, the railroad looked like an expensive, evaporating dream until China undertook to build it. The *Nationalist*, the official daily paper of the Tanganyika African National Union, was lavish with its praise:

"Here, the continent is breaking with her past as she enters a new historical stage—the stage of national reconstruction and intensified national liberation struggle to build a new Africa free of imperialist oppression and exploitation. Here, Africa is asserting her right, thanks to the genuine internationalism of the Chinese people, of access to the domain of world technology which her oppressors have always denied her . . . "

There were nearly five thousand Chinese in Tanzania when construction was started on the railroad; the number rose steadily as the work progressed.

Chinese military advisors were assigned at the same time to the Tanzanian army. Two months earlier, the Chinese had started work on a base in Dar es Salaam for the small fleet of naval patrol boats the Chinese were furnishing the Tanzanians. Still earlier, the Chinese had taken over the training functions at the police school in Moshi.

Chinese soldiers had also been assigned as instructors in the Tanzanian bases of a dozen liberation movements that were plotting insurrections in Portuguese Mozambique or Rhodesia or South Africa. Some of these groups made frequent raids into their white-dominated homelands in southern Africa, or conducted steady guerrilla warfare there.

Tanzania had become the main supply route for Chinese weapons that were transported to Black Africa, although not all the weapons were put in the hands of the Tanzanian army or the rebels fighting the white-dominated south. A rebellion in the Congo was kept alive by weapons sent across Tanzania by rail from Dar es Salaam to Kigoma. A convoy of weapons bound for Uganda from Tanzania was intercepted by police in Kenya, arousing the anger and suspicion of President Kenyatta. President Hastings Kamuzu Banda of Malawi, who sought to come to some sort of accommodation with the white rulers in the south, accused President Nyerere of permitting a rebellion to be plotted in Tanzania against his government, too. Even the Watusi, who spent years bogged down in an attempt to invade Rwanda from Burundi and Tanzania, had been armed with Chinese weapons.

Many of these weapons drifted around the continent, being sold or bartered among bands of rebels, thieves, poachers and others. The weapons traffic was hard to control in so vast and primitive a country as Tanzania, with too few roads and little else in the way of communication, with borders on eight countries, some of which were in a fairly constant state of revolutionary ferment. Some of Tanzania's neighbors worried that the huge caldron of potential trouble around that country might one day bubble up and spill over onto everyone.

The Western powers fretted, too. They had hoped for a gradual, orderly process of adjustments and realignments in East Africa after independence, and had not expected that China would be imbedded so quickly. A Chinese base in Tanzania would have a wide periphery in Africa, and would give China a foothold on the western shore of the Indian Ocean.

Nyerere bristled at suggestions that China might gain a position of strength in Africa through her influence in Tanzanian affairs. The President insisted that Tanzania would be nobody's puppet. After formally opening a French-built cotton textile mill in Mwanza in 1969, he said: "We are a stubborn people. The Chinese will learn that if they want to control us they will get into trouble."

Nyerere was a zealous pan-Africanist. He was committed to the overthrow of white rule in Africa, and searched for means to make the guerrilla wars against the whites in the south more effective. If the Chinese, who were willing to build the railroad he wanted, were willing to train the guerrillas, all Nyerere's principles demanded that he should let them. If the Chinese had some suggestions for improving the lot of the Tanzanians, and Nyerere felt the suggestions were good ones, it was fitting that he should let them try. He had always said he wanted simply to get the best deal he could for his country. In all these things he had been consistent.

"We use every possible weapon against our poverty," Nyerere had said in 1965 at a state banquet in Dar es Salaam for Chou En-lai, the visiting Chinese premier. But then Nyerere added, as though in warning:

"From no quarter shall we accept direction or neocolonialism and at no time shall we lower our guard against the subversion of our government. Neither our principles, our country nor our freedom to determine our own future are for sale."

The railroad project was still in the talking stage then, as were many other Chinese projects, but technical help from the Chinese, and loans and gifts and cultural visits and other things had already begun to exceed by far what the Tanzanians had been getting from anyone else.

The Chinese helped set up a joint shipping line with Chinese-built freighters; the Tanzanians got an interest-free loan from the Chinese to pay for their half, and were told they did not have to start paying until after ten years, and then only from their share of the profits of the shipping line.

The Chinese built a textile mill for the Tanzanians at Ubungo, near Dar es Salaam, and permitted the Tanzanians to pay for it with another interest-free Chinese loan. Ironically, the water needed for the mill's operation was drawn from an American

*Anti-apartheid demonstrations in Dar es Salaam, 1965*

*A Chinese acrobatic team performs in Dar es Salaam*

project that had been started before, to increase Dar es Salaam's overtaxed water resources.

The Chinese also gave the Tanzanians a shortwave transmitting station at Mabibo, near Dar es Salaam, with the same easy financing arrangement. Before long, the Tanzanians were beaming broadcasts even in Afrikaans to the Boers of South Africa.

A wide variety of gifts and shows were provided by the Chinese, including an experimental farm, a marine police force, bicycles, cash, cars, folk-dancing shows, teams of Chinese physicians on loan, portraits of Mao Tse-tung, even a bookshop and a snack bar for the University College.

President Kenneth Kaunda of Zambia was reluctant at first to accept the Chinese offer to build the railroad, but changed his mind when he failed to stir any real commitment to the project

in Britain, France, West Germany or the United States. He wanted
to free his country from its humiliating dependence on the life-
lines through Rhodesia and the Portuguese territories of Angola
and Mozambique.

"If Mars offered money to build the railway we would take it,"
Kaunda said in 1965.

Nyerere was less worried about the political implications of
bringing in the Chinese in large numbers. He had always argued
that big slices of Communist aid would help offset the old pre-
ponderance of the West in his country.

He had approached the Russians about the railroad, and was
turned down. The World Bank had been approached, but it
advised the Africans that the line would be uneconomic in the
foreseeable future, and that it would be far cheaper to improve
the existing roads, railroads and ports, including those through
the white-controlled south.

The report disappointed the Zambian and Tanzanian leaders.
It offered the Chinese an obvious diplomatic opening, for the
Zambians felt the World Bank's solution would leave them hos-
tage to the governments of southern Africa.

Eventually the Zambians accepted the offer the Chinese had
made to Nyerere when he visited China in 1965. As the terms
were worked out finally, China agreed to finance the railroad
project with a $412 million, interest-free loan that was to be
shared equally by Zambia and Tanzania, and paid back over a
period of thirty years beginning in 1983. In other words, it was
practically a gift; no Western government or credit institution
could have matched the terms and called it anything less than a
gift.

At a time when relations among the three East African countries were deteriorating, the Chinese offer to build the railroad
had great significance. It strengthened the growing association of
Kaunda and Nyerere. Both their countries bordered on white-
governed states. Kaunda wanted an outlet to the sea through the
black north, and trading connections with the black north instead of the white south. Nyerere welcomed the prospect of in-
creased trade and enhanced prestige, and the opportunity to

have Dar es Salaam transformed into a bigger port. He also wanted to open up the untouched mineral and agricultural resources that lay in the rugged southern regions along the line of rail.

Another strain on the ties with Kenya and Uganda came from Nyerere's disappointment that neither Kenyatta nor Obote had followed his lead in 1965 in breaking relations with Britain; the break had been proposed by the Organization of African Unity, to show Africa's pique over Britain's reluctance to use troops in Rhodesia, to reassert her authority in that colony after its white-minority government proclaimed its independence.

Speaking later at Morogoro Teachers' College, Nyerere said it was time that some African countries made up their minds whether to give priority to their association with their former colonial masters, or to Africa. He was shocked, he said, to see that some newly independent states in Africa had sent representatives to the Organization of African Unity with credentials signed by the old colonial powers.

"I cannot understand this," Nyerere said. "Africa must really be in a big mess and I think there is a devil somewhere causing all this confusion. I am a good superstitious African who believes in devils and there must be a devil in Africa."

President Obote of Uganda eventually grew to be more militant in pan-African politics, and to bait the British more readily. His behavior changed partly in order to offer Ugandans a diversion from their troubled internal politics; partly because Obote felt Uganda could not stand without other allies in an association with Kenya. Uganda was too vulnerable; her lifeline to the coast, the railroad to Mombasa, ran through Kenya, and in a serious argument with Kenya that lifeline could always be squeezed, or pinched shut.

Obote looked to Nyerere for support, and increasingly to President Kaunda of Zambia. The three of them met often, and called their informal association the Mulungushi Club, named after the place in Zambia where Kaunda always held his party's national conferences.

Rules of thumb that describe African leaders as pro-communist or pro-capitalist, or as leaning in one direction or the other, as moderate or reactionary or progressive, have never stood up for long. It is difficult to categorize any of them, especially Obote. His air force was trained by Czech and Israeli pilots at the same time, and was equipped with jets from Israel and from the Soviet Union. The army was equipped partly with Chinese rifles.

Kenyatta's standing as an African nationalist was unassailable, but he was suspicious of both his neighboring East African leaders because of their abusive public treatment of Britain and because of their dealings with the Chinese. In 1965, soon after Chou En-lai left Dar es Salaam, Kenyatta spoke at a public rally at Nairobi about the nature of independence. It was the season of the "long rains" in East Africa, but the warm African sun streamed down unexpectedly on tens of thousands who gathered to hear him:

"For over forty years I fought and sacrificed my active life so that this country could get rid of the yoke of colonialism and imperialism. Many sons and daughters of our land suffered and shed blood so that our children may be born free. You can, therefore, understand my personal feelings about the future. How can I tolerate anything that could compromise or jeopardize the promise to our children?" Kenyatta asked.

"It is true that we have passed through many years of Western imperialism. It is natural that we should detest Western colonialism, and associate the word imperialism with the West. But if we are truly non-aligned we must not avoid making friends with those Western countries who extend an honest field of cooperation and trade.

"To do this would be to prove that we are not free and cannot separate good from bad. It would prove that we still suffer from a colonial mentality.

"It is naive to think that there is no danger of imperialism from the East," he said. "Kenya shall not exchange one master for a new master."

Kenyatta had sought, as had the other East African leaders, to avoid being dragged into the fringes of the cold war, the arena of struggle for the giant powers of the world.

But it was there. As work on the Chinese railroad progressed, the Americans speeded up the improvements they had been making to the old Great North Road that ran over roughly the same route, straightening it and paving the stretches that had caused truck drivers to name it "Hell Run."

All day long and through the night, trucks rumbled over the road, sometimes alone, sometimes in long convoys, carrying copper out of Zambia, and other supplies back down from Dar es Salaam. For the most part, especially in the high, rugged stretches in southern Tanzania, the road had been a miserable, dangerous trail, unpaved and often washed away, climbing in places along treacherous escarpments. It presented the whole range of African driving hazards from dust and mud to families of snarling baboons.

Scores of businesses were quickly established along the road as it came into heavy use. Most typical of them was the African-owned *hoteli*, not so much a hotel as a dark little cafe that offered beer or tea and cheap African food.

A bed for the night could also be had in some of them, but the truck drivers took pride in and could earn more money by working in pairs to keep their vehicles on the move, with one man at the wheel and the other taking a nap on the high ledge at the back of the cab behind the driver.

The road project and the railroad, even when both were in the very first stages of work, developed into a kind of cold war competition: the railroad as a sign of Chinese generosity and abiding interest in East Africa, and the road project as a demonstration of American speed and practicality.

For the East Africans it might have been an amusing spectacle, a show from which they stood to gain something from each side. But in East Africa there is a proverb that everyone knows: "When elephants fight it is the grass that suffers."

# CHAPTER 9

# THE QUIET REVOLUTION

For centuries East Africa has been history's victim. The slave trade, the journeys of discovery, the missionary conversions and colonization had an enormous impact on the people.

Their patterns of life and their forms of traditional culture have been shattered or fragmented or ignored by the hurrying outside world. They are caught in the fringes of a strange culture that seems uncomprehending and sometimes cruel, with an alien religion, alien language, alien patterns of thought.

Some Africans come to terms with it. Some are drawn to it and overwhelmed by it, and these poor people can be seen in Nairobi, Kampala, Dar es Salaam and in all the bigger towns—unemployed, wandering, asleep in the parks or standing on the corners, waiting for something to happen.

They are rudderless and bewildered people, living in a world they feel someone else has created, measuring themselves by the standards of others, wearing shoes that pinch and clothes that have been designed for other climates. Sometimes their anger and humiliation boil over.

*A Kikuyu tribes-
man on his first
visit to Nairobi*

"Youths in Europe are frustrated," declared Joseph Nyerere at a rally in Dar es Salaam of Tanzania's Youth League early in 1968 when this anger and humiliation began to seethe in Tanzania. His brother, President Julius Nyerere, called the league his "Green Guards," and entrusted it with the task of leading the country's cultural revolution.

"Now we seem to want to imitate the way they behave, even the way they smile," Joseph Nyerere said at the rally, ridiculing the urge among Africans to copy European ways. "We will eradicate such illusions. Our youths will not be strangers in their own country."

The Green Guards started out to clear Tanzania of miniskirts, wigs, skin bleaches, hair straighteners and trousers that hugged the hips or were very tight or had flared bottoms or were fitted with wide belts.

They pulled girls off the buses in Kariakoo Market, and beat them and ripped off their clothes if their skirts were too short. In Mwanza, men were allowed to pass unmolested only if their trousers were wide enough so that a beer bottle would fit up the pants leg.

The cultural revolution spread to Zanzibar, where the government imposed a three months' prison sentence for miniskirt wearers. In Uganda a campaign was begun by younger members of the Uganda People's Congress, but the party hierarchy stopped them.

In Tanzania, meanwhile, the cultural revolution had gone off on an erratic new course. Students at the University College demanded that all their American teachers be expelled; military law was being added to the curriculum and the students claimed that their research papers would expose Tanzania's military secrets to the "enemy."

By 1970 some militant Tanzanians were denouncing the bushy "Afro" hair style of young American blacks as a product of that white, Western world from which Africans were trying to free themselves. It was a shock to the small colony of black Americans living in Tanzania to see the "Afro" portrayed as a symbol of American decadence.

The black Americans who picked up the style had wanted to celebrate their African heritage rather than mimic white fashion by straightening their hair. They let it grow out, even encouraged it to look wild and bushy, to accent their African heritage.

But the men and women in Kenya, Uganda and Tanzania usually cropped their hair short and the women covered their shorn heads with bandanas. Deep in the interior, close to the Congo border, the women let their hair grow long, but braided it into stiff strands that arched upward in a variety of configurations.

The women in East Africa who wore the "Afro" hairdo picked it up from America, not from Africa. To the militant young Africans, it was another sign of the cultural invasion, as were soul music and minis, maxis and midis.

Even the Masai, the tribesmen who wandered with their tiny, humpbacked cattle over the vast plains below Kilimanjaro, fell victim to the cultural revolution for showing too much bare buttock under their traditional *shukas* and for not wearing trousers —in other words, for not adapting to dress that had its origins in the West.

When the Masai persisted in wearing *shukas*, hundreds were arrested. The Masai herdsman depicted on the 100 shilling Tanzanian banknote was removed from it by the Tanzanian parliament because of "his disgraceful attire." Finally the Masai were banned from buses and other forms of public transport unless they were in Western clothes. Green Guards rushed from one bus to another to enforce the ban.

The Green Guards who pulled one Masai tribesman off a bus near Arusha were laughing and screaming to the point of hysteria. The doctors who treated some of the Green Guards with sedatives said the cases were not unlike the hysteria experienced by schoolgirls in Bwiri, Geita, Bunda, Musoma and Mwanza, and other such places. In each of those cases the children had started laughing and crying and dancing in a frenzied, uncontrollable way. It has been suggested that the children had not been able to cope with the contradictions between their village life and the modern environment of school. Feeling they could be censured by either for failing to measure up, they rejected both. In their own minds, they were waiting for something better, and within reach.

H. W. O. Okoth Ogendo, when he was a law student in Dar es Salaam University College, put in verse his feeling that much

*Masai warriors at Kajiado, Kenya*

of the old had to be destroyed before an undisturbed new
African consciousness could be aroused. In "Flames of Consciousness," he wrote:

> . . . Then will come the cry
> that kindles the flames of destruction
> Eating deep and sharply
> into the core of our existence.
> To live,
> To die,
> To be born again—

Perhaps the transition would have been easier if more had been
understood about the Africans, or if more people had cared about
their ways. Missionaries and colonizers had seen their role, at
best, as a kind of cultural, economic and religious rescue operation. There was no effort to save what was African in Africa
because, in the eyes of the intruders, there was nothing worth
saving. Sir Philip Mitchell, a British governor of Kenya when it
was a colony, described what the colonizers had found:

"The West found itself in control of millions of people who
had never invented or adopted an alphabet or even any form of
hieroglyphic writing. They had no numerals, no almanac or calendar, no notation of time or measurements of length, capacity, or
weight, no currency, no external trade except slaves and ivory
. . . no plough, no wheel and no means of transportation except
human head porterage on land and dugout canoes on rivers and
lakes. These people had built nothing, nothing of any kind, in any
material more durable than mud, poles, and thatch. With a few
notable exceptions, there were no units of government throughout
the area larger than the tribe, and the tribe might amount only to
a few thousand people and have half a dozen contending chiefs
. . . Great numbers wore no clothes at all; others wore bark
cloth or hides and skins."

It was a harsh judgment of the Africans, one that did not take
into account their oral traditions, their exciting and earthy re-
ligions, their innate politeness, their cheerfulness in the worst

adversity, their deep sense of personal responsibility to family and tribe.

The missionaries condemned pagan marriages and polygamy. They ignored the significance of families and clans in marriage. They introduced the white wedding gown, the veil and the ring to marriages, all symbols that meant nothing to Africans. Among the customs that meant more to them were the forced but good-natured fattening of the bride, or the shaving and braiding of her hair or the custom of giving the bride stones for her fireplace.

Very often the Africans looked upon Christianity in a white mission as a desirable item of Western equipment, something to be acquired as a sign of progress, with about the same sense of pride and accomplishment as a school uniform, or a bar of soap, or a transistor radio, or eyeglasses—with or without glass in them.

Africans were still, long after independence, being given names at baptism like Patrick, Robert, Maria, Daniel and others with r's and l's that the Bantu people do not distinguish between in their speech. They often dropped the names as soon as they were away from the mission station and among their own people, and used the African names they got at birth.

In spite of their good works—the hospitals and the schools—the missionaries were often among the first to suffer violence when the thin veneer of order broke down.

In spite of the stained-glass windows and the expensive organs, Africans drifted away from the established churches to set up their own open-air churches, and to conduct their own services and sing their hymns to the rhythm of drums.

In his inaugural address to the Tanganyika parliament on December 10, 1962, President Nyerere expressed wonder that foreigners did not see that a man could be moved more deeply by his own traditional art forms than by anything foreign, even if his art be nothing more than shaking pebbles in a tin can:

"Of all the crimes of colonialism there is none worse than the attempt to make us believe we had no indigenous culture of our own; or that what we did have was worthless—something of which we should be ashamed, instead of a source of pride. Some of us, particularly those of us who acquired a European type of education, set ourselves out to prove to our colonial rulers that we had become civilized; and by that we meant that we had abandoned everything connected with our own past and learned to imitate only European ways. Our young men's ambition was not to become well-educated Africans but to become Black Europeans! Indeed, at one time it was a compliment rather than an insult to call a man who imitated the Europeans a 'Black European'—*Mzungu Mweusi.*"

Tom Mboya, the Kenya cabinet minister who was assassinated in 1969, wondered how many white people could appreciate how an African felt going through the course of his education reading books about Zeus and Saturn instead of Ngai or Lwanda Magere, or about King Arthur instead of Gor Mahia or Odera Akang'o, or about boars and wolves instead of lions and giraffes.

Daniel arap Moi, who was Kenya's vice-president, asked rhetorically in a speech in Nakuru in 1967 why Africans had to be taught that Lake Victoria was discovered by Speke. Africans knew the lake was there; its discovery was not recorded by Africans any more than was the discovery of the English Channel by the ancient Britons and Gauls. Milton Obote, when he was still President of Uganda, registered another complaint when he spoke at the Makerere Arts Festival in 1968:

"Some years ago, when I was a student at Makerere, I read something about daffodils. I think it was a poem, and I found myself in the miserable situation of trying to write an appreciation of the poem, for I had never seen a daffodil."

There were alternatives to becoming a *Mzungu Mweusi,* just as there had long been angry reactions to such things as the lessons about bears and wolves and daffodils. There was anti-imperialism, anti-colonialism, anti-neocolonialism, African Socialism, the cultural revolution. Some of it was mere slogan-inventing, but some of it was real.

In the 1930's a movement called negritude began as an attempt to sum up the art and literature and other cultural values of the black world. Léopold Sédar Senghor, who was a poet and presi-

*A Kikuyu boy in tribal dress shakes hands with the groom at Tom Mboya's wedding in Nairobi in 1962*

dent of Senegal, was a great advocate of the movement and said in *Optima* in March 1966 that negritude was no different from the "black personality" discovered and proclaimed by blacks in America.

Negritude began with people from French West Africa living in Paris, but it spread to East Africa, just as it spread in another direction to the West Indies, with undiminished fury and passion. Aimé Césaire, one of its leading figures, wrote in *Return to My Native Land:*

> my Negritude is not a stone, its deafness
>     thrown against the clamor of the day
> my Negritude is not a speck of dead water
>     on the dead eye of earth
> my Negritude is neither a tower nor a
>     cathedral
> it thrusts into the red flesh of the soil
> it thrusts into the warm flesh of the sky
> it digs under the opaque dejection
>     of its rightful patience

The negritude movement was born in France and its writers worked in the French language. Part of the reason for the frustration among Africans was that they could not speak to one another, outside the limited circle of their own tribes, except in English or French or Portuguese. Of all the imperialistic forces, language was the least visible and the most effective in the long run. But without it, there would have been no word for any Bantu to use for cathedral or pillowcase or steel. There would have been no books, or written poetry. In French, Césaire vented his anger against his people, and against people like Sir Philip Mitchell, the former Kenya governor who may have judged the Africans too quickly. Elsewhere in his poem, Césaire wrote of:

> those who have invented neither gunpowder
>     nor compass
> those who tamed neither steam nor electricity
> those who explored neither the sea nor the sky

> but those without whom the earth would not
> be the earth

There was another alternative to becoming a *Mzungu Mweusi*.
Jaramogi Oginga Odinga, who later was to become the opposition
leader in Kenya, set the pattern for it in the Kenya legislative
council when he walked in one day, much to the distress of some
of his colleagues, in a brand new "traditional" dress that included
a beaded cap, a fine beaded goatskin apron and a fly whisk.

The real traditional dress of Odinga's Luo tribe was less expensive, at least as late as the opening of the Uganda Railroad.
The Duke and Duchess of Connaught visited the terminal at
Kisumu then, in the Luo part of Kenya. A British official, wanting
to spare the Duchess any embarrassment, issued a yard of calico
to each of the local residents. It was a hot day and when the
train steamed into the terminal, a huge crowd stood waiting to
see the brother of the king. Everyone in the crowd was wearing
the cloth not around his middle, but around his head.

Farther along the shore of Lake Victoria the traditional dress
was longer established than Odinga's, but not more African. The
Muganda man's traditional dress was a *kanzu*, a long robe of the
sort introduced by Arab slave traders, but worn over a suit of
Western clothes. The Muganda woman's traditional dress was a
*busuti*, a long, flowing dress, bunched at the waist and with
butterfly shoulders; it had been introduced in Victorian times by
an English schoolteacher.

As the end of British rule in East Africa approached, national
dress took on a new importance, as did legends. Where legends
did not exist, the Africans cheerfully invented them as they went
along, adding flavor to their own special, moving world.

Almost nothing that had been left to them was their own.
Even their national borders had been set out not by them and
not by the course of history in East Africa alone, but by per-
spiring white men peering through theodolites, concerned more
about the balance of power in Europe than about Africa.

African politicians had mounted the world stage, and after
the first few years, nobody listened. African farmers planted

*Muganda women, in traditional dress,*
*watch the building of a new highway*

more coffee, tea, cotton, sisal and a lot of other crops they had
been taught to grow, and the prices went down. African nations
absorbed great quantities of economic aid, and still the gap grew
wider between themselves and their foreign benefactors. African
sympathy and aid for the liberation struggles against the white-
dominated south of Africa had come to naught. All three East
African countries suffered the humiliating experience after independence of having to call back British troops to put down army
mutinies. Africans wanted at least to get some measure of control
over the speed and direction in which they were being taken, but
they could not do this quickly.

Seth Adagala, appointed in 1968 to set up a Kenya National
Theater, said he did not mind accepting help from white people
and using Shakespearean texts. He felt confident that a truly
African theater would come in time.

"It's not the form that matters," he said. "We can absorb
techniques, and make original use of them. We want to be enriched without being swamped. We want to learn. Anyway, it's
only a beginning."

In all the cities of East Africa, the Africans were great window-
shoppers. They did not often have the money to go inside the
shops, but they stood and stared, studying sometimes for hours
the prices and goods in the windows and all that went on inside.

They streamed into the cities, forsaking the security of life in
the village to endure or enjoy the impersonal, adventurous life
of the glittering big towns. Work and life in towns anyplace in
the world have always had a character of their own, and the
Africans found the adjustment especially hard.

In their own tribal environments, everything in their daily
routine and behavior was prescribed for the Africans, from the
time they were infants to the time they should have been ancestor-
spirits. No one escaped his rigidly organized social obligations.
No one was considered a fully developed human until he had
grown to understand his role in this tight society. The Zulu are
credited with a saying: *"Umuntu ungumuntu nga bantu"*—"Man
is man because of men." The saying spread to many Bantu

languages, for it expresses the reality of man's condition in this process of gradually learning cultural behavior and of learning to play a role in the social group.

In the city it was different. The city was a place of individuals, dreamers, venturers, unconcerned people, treacherous friends, tricksters, women looking for an easier life or one offering more excitement than did their traditional jobs of bearing children and tilling the soil.

A Swahili song called *"Rosa Umekuwa Mshamba,"* meaning "Rosa Has Become a Country Girl," made the rounds in Tanzania

*Shoppers in Nairobi*

soon after independence, particularly in villages in the interior. It was a plaintive tune, telling how much better off and happier Rosa might have been had she packed her bags and moved into town. It was so popular that it threatened almost by itself to wreck President Nyerere's attempts to get people out of Dar es Salaam and back to the land.

The flow of people to the towns put an enormous burden on the new states of East Africa. The towns and cities did not have industry and commerce on the scale needed to absorb the new-comers without agony and dislocation. There were not enough jobs, not enough houses and often not enough essential services like water, power and sanitation.

This migration created problems not only for governments, but for people to whom life in the city was a whole new way of living. It was not unusual for an African with a wife and one way of life in the city to try to spend two or three days a week with another wife and another way of life in the village. Many an African lost his job in the city for absenteeism or for not paying attention to his work. Many an African searched his soul in an effort to determine to which world he really belonged. Some could never find out, as Lennard Okola, a Kenyan poet, suggested in a passage from "A Voice in the Dark":

> I told my soul,
> come out into the open
> that the world may see you
> and make your acquaintance,
> but my soul replied
> waving a white handkerchief:
> "the world will never know me
> for I don't know myself,
> I have only seen my face
> through a broken mirror
> in a bathroom filled with steam;
> I have only seen myself
> dancing with the ripples
> in a muddy pond after a torrent."

# CHAPTER 10

# THE FUTURE

The exhilarating mood of *Uhuru* was captured eloquently by Julius Nyerere in 1961, when he sent an expedition to plant a flag and a burning torch atop Kilimanjaro, the highest peak in Africa, and said: "It will shine beyond our borders, giving hope where there was despair, love where there was hate, and dignity where before there was only humiliation."

Some of the dreams of *Uhuru* were shattered soon afterward. A very few have been fulfilled. In the wake of the disappointments, a more realistic outlook has arisen, along with new hopes for genuine progress.

The East Africans need hope and very clear vision in order to see a better future for themselves; their shortcomings after independence were all too easily seen. The people lack the skills that would have enabled them to improve and take control of their own economies quickly. They need to know more about hygiene and preventive medicine.

One of the commonest tragic sights in East Africa is that of children who are getting food to eat, but are starving nonetheless.

Their heads are tufted with gray hair, their skin is light-colored and blotchy, their stomachs swollen, their legs bent and spindly. They are old enough to walk or crawl, but do not. Neither do they laugh, nor brush away the flies that settle on their lips and in the corners of their eyes.

They are victims of kwashiorkor, the protein-deficiency disease that Africans call "the sickness the old baby gets when the new baby comes." It is chronic and pervasive in East Africa and the way to cure it is by teaching the mothers what to feed their children so that they get the protein they need.

Frequently there are years of real starvation, when the rains fail and expanses of grazing land wither to bare earth. The Africans dig holes in the dry riverbeds then, looking for water for their cattle. When they find no water, they kill the cattle for food. When they have no cattle, they eat the leaves of the *mopani* tree or caterpillars or the grubs they find under rocks. When they have neither cattle nor grain for too long a time, they die.

The specter of famine looms always near. Yet with help the East Africans will learn to store their grain longer, to plant a wider variety of drought-resistant crops, and not keep so many cattle that their pastures are grazed too closely and ruined. The people will learn more about conserving and storing water by building dams and weirs and irrigation schemes that are scaled to their needs and to their means.

They need roads to the remotest areas so that all African farmers can grow produce for market. They need surveys of their natural resources, not only of mineral deposits and waterways that could be made to produce power, but of the land; if the soils were analyzed and the rainfall and temperatures and hours of sunlight were measured, crops could be planted wisely in the most suitable places.

All three East African countries are trying to rely less on foreign aid. None of them has the funds or the skills to realize its ambitious plans alone, but foreign aid is too often tied to imported goods, leaving the East Africans to dig for additional funds to meet the local costs of the projects. Too often to suit the Africans, aid is tied to specific projects and foreigners are thereby determin-

*A mobile health clinic visits a rural region of Tanzania*

ing the priorities for much of the development the Africans want.
The usefulness of foreign aid is easily exaggerated; the importance of the Africans' own efforts is too easily overlooked.

In Kenya, Tanzania and Uganda strenuous efforts are being
made to broaden the economies so they will be less heavily dependent on one or two basic export commodities, for the Africans

have almost no control over the prices their commodities fetch, and are at the mercy of vague, unstable world markets.

At the time of independence, Tanganyika and sisal were almost synonymous, but within half a dozen years, mainly because of competition from synthetic fibers, the prices for sisal were a third of what they had been. In Kenya, coffee prices sagged for years after independence, and then coffee berry disease swept over the country, ruining hundreds of growers. Uganda was dependent on her coffee and cotton exports, and was hit by the slumping prices for both commodities.

It is clear that new sources of income have to be found for the future, and in all three countries a good start has been made. Half-used or badly used grasslands have been opened up to ranching. New crops have been introduced and new markets for the grains and beef found in Arabia and Europe and the Far East. The peasant farmers are turning increasingly to producing crops for market.

Still, people stream into the towns looking for work. To many young people, especially the ones who have been to school, opportunity seems to lie in the westernized cities, however overcrowded they are. The association of education with superior employment is deeply engraved in the minds of Africans; to them, education seems to be the key to the white man's magic.

But in East Africa, the white man's education system has created expectations without a corresponding chance of fulfillment. The system produced many literate people, but after independence populations rose faster than new schools could be built. Too few of those finishing primary school can find places in secondary schools. Of those who finish secondary school, there is not room for everyone in a university. For those who finish university, there is still too little choice of jobs.

The system breeds resentment and this might have been expected, as Arthur T. Porter, the principal of University College in Nairobi, put it in 1968: "What defense can we make for a system if its only result seems to be its success in taking a child out of the farm to the town where he cannot find employment?"

This disenchantment stirs the whole tangle of problems that

beset the new governments: unemployment, social rootlessness, crime, family disintegration. None of the problems is unique to East Africa, but they are felt severely, and are especially unsettling to these young states struggling to find their feet.

Even in the villages there is discontent over education, so keen are the Africans for it. In Kenya, the government encouraged a system of Harambee Schools, where everyone was expected to pull together. The villagers put up the buildings. The schools

*An irrigation program brings water to a dry area in northeast Kenya*

were then to be staffed and equipped by the government, but the government could not find enough teachers.

In Tanzania, President Nyerere reasoned that if education were ever to be made relevant to Tanzania's agricultural way of life, the place to start was at the primary school desk. He wanted to shape the courses of study around the future scientific farmers rather than the Latin scholars, because most of Tanzania's pupils would have to return to the land.

Also, because the pupils coming out of primary school were only twelve or thirteen years old, not old enough to be responsible workers and citizens and with too little chance to continue their education, Nyerere determined that children should not be started in school until they were eight years old; that way, if they could not go on to secondary school they would at least be old enough to work.

"These are the economic facts of life for our country," he wrote in a policy paper in 1967. "They are the practical meaning of our poverty."

The reforms he sought were slow to be accepted and to begin taking effect; education is still too widely regarded as a necessary prerequisite to position and wealth.

"Bad things do not disappear because we pretend they are not there, or because we accuse other people of causing them," Nyerere said later.

"Complaining that we are poor, or that world prices are low, is as useless as complaining that the rains do not fall. We have to assess our present situation—which includes many things beyond our control—and work out plans to change the situation and counteract the effect of the things we cannot alter. Then we have to execute our plans by hard and intelligent work. There is no other way. There is no short cut."

East Africa's potential resources have to be exploited in the meantime, however, with foreign help.

Kenyatta kept British advisors and technicians in his government as long as they could not be replaced by Africans. He encouraged the white settlers to stay on their farms in the highlands, and promised that they would not have to sell until they wanted to and had time to get the prices they sought. The Indian merchants, the *duka-wallahs* so cordially disliked by so many Africans, could stay if they had become citizens or otherwise identified themselves with the country, or performed some really needed service. Even the missionaries were welcome to stay, and one of Kenyatta's earliest recollections had been of missionaries causing his father to be taken to jail as a witch doctor.

"My father's calabashes were taken as evidence of guilt, and

*Students of Kenya's Animal Health and Industry Training Institute examine a newborn calf*

he, with many others in the same position, served a period of imprisonment," Kenyatta wrote in his book, *Facing Mount Kenya.*

The witch doctors came into their own after independence. Not only missionaries but many others had overlooked the importance Africans attach to their own religion and philosophy of life. An integral part of this is the witch doctor. He can provide useful herbal cures, and the Africans have faith in him. The white man's medicine is accepted for its quick cures, its helpful injections, its emergency operations, for its treatment of illnesses that can be identified easily and have a start and an end. But for the African with some vague, persisting pain, the witch doctor's advice is usually sought first, and will continue to be sought for

a long time ahead. The wiser doctors and witch doctors are learning to accommodate to each other's views and experiences. Not
all the witch doctors' herbal remedies are hocus-pocus. And as
psychologists, some of the witch doctors are superb.

Much as doctors and witch doctors are learning to work side
by side, so are the established churches, whether Roman Catholic,
Protestant or Orthodox, fundamentalist or high church or other,
learning to accommodate to the Africans' longing for services
and rituals they can feel and understand. As a result, whole
denominational patterns have been altered.

Old liturgies brought by missionaries from Europe and the
United States no longer seem to suit the spiritual needs of many
Africans. In their place, Africans are creating new religious practices or tailoring old practices to their experiences, and the
established churches are going along. The churches are accepting
not merely drums and whistles instead of organ music, but basic
changes that would once have been unthinkable, even the baptism of wives of polygamous marriages.

The Reverend Gabriel Kmotho, a Kikuyu and a Roman Catholic
priest in Nairobi, explained why he could not withhold baptism
from such women when they wanted it:

"My mother was the second wife. Could I say to her that she
was living in sin? Could I say that to my father?

"When someone would ask my father, 'Where is your wife?' he
would say, 'Oh, I don't have only one wife. Which wife do you
mean? They are all my wives. I love them. I am responsible for
all my children.'"

Another problem for East Africans is to learn to live with their
booming business of tourism. It means preserving their wildlife on
vast tracts of grazing land so that foreigners can watch a
rhinoceros charging aimlessly across a shimmering plain, a pride
of lions asleep in the tall grass or an elephant playfully uprooting
a tree. It means allowing herds of zebra and wildebeest to roam at
will, and leaving potentially useful fields in nature's cover of thorn
trees and bush and the occasional color-splashed bed of wild-
flowers.

The East African leaders appreciate the money tourism earns

*Lions at rest in Nairobi National Park, Kenya*

and the jobs it provides, and a conscious effort is made in each
of these countries to make visitors feel comfortable and welcome.
The authorities try to keep their cattleherding people from over-
grazing and ruining land that is of only marginal value to them.
The authorities discourage the poachers who kill wastefully and
cruelly with snares; some of them want the elephant only for
his ivory or the rhino only for his "aphrodisiac" horn, and leave
the flesh to be eaten by predators or to rot in the relentless
African sun.

Poachers are not loved by conservationists, nor by big game
hunters who shoot for the thrill of it or for trophies. But poachers
most often hunt animals only for meat, as their forebears have
done for generations. They have little wish to yield their prior

claim to the animals to foreigners who merely look from the comfort and security of a lodge or a bus. This was the general theme of "The Poacher's Lament," a poem by Okumu pa'Lukobo, a Ugandan:

> If, boy, you had to choose
> Between an animal to gape at
> And meat in a bowl to eat
> Which in your hunger would you take?

In the early years after independence, the East African leader perhaps most openly concerned about preserving wildlife and its natural habitat was President Nyerere. Even his concern was not immediate and deeply felt, to judge from a remark he made to a group of foreigners who told him how impressed they were by the scenery of Serengeti. Nyerere replied that the words took him back to his college days in Scotland, where people praised the beauty of the moorlands and the heather.

"I did not agree then either, but I decided it meant something to you which I would never understand," he said.

The first concern of these leaders must be their people, and the people treasure their livestock and the soil, not the wild animals. Most often, Africans regard the wild animals around them as beasts to be hunted for the meat they yield, or to be driven away for damaging their crops or threatening their herds of goats or cattle. The slopes and plains are to be grazed or, if the soil is good and the water plentiful, to be planted with corn and beans and some crops to sell as well. Kenyatta's preoccupation is with such practical matters, as he made clear once in a talk at Machakos after independence:

"I love the soil and I love those who love the soil," he said. "The soil has knit us together . . . it is our greatest investment . . . other things come and go, but well-cultivated soil remains. The soil has been there from the beginning of time . . . soil is the mother of wealth, development and general prosperity."

The people and the soil remain East Africa's most important assets after independence, and the greatest hope for the area. In the undernourished economies of Kenya, Uganda and Tanzania, the most dynamic new factor is the poor, untrained peasant farmer. He is the one for whom the least planning can be done, and for whom the least immediate help is available. He is eager to learn. Through sheer enthusiasm and the discovery that hard work can be rewarding, he is causing dramatic rises in production for many crops, some for export and some for the markets of Nairobi, Kampala and Dar es Salaam.

The farmer is also most receptive to the arguments that industrial development need not be on a grand scale, but ought to be achieved through small factories that will produce farm tools or process food or otherwise suit an expanding agricultural economy. These are the tools he needs, and the factories that can process the food he grows. He understands that these developments can bring about a quick and direct improvement in his lot.

If there is disappointment in the rate of progress, it is because hopes were set unrealistically high. As long as there is disappointment, there is the chance that East Africa will boil up and spill

*A farmer sprays his cotton crop on newly settled land in the foothills of the Ruwenzori Mountains in Uganda*

over periodically. A way still must be found to provide for peaceful changes of government. General Amin's coup in Uganda is a reminder that if political leaders get too entrenched or too deep in trouble, the army is there as a means of removing them. None of the governments in East Africa can be secure until the quiet revolution has run its course. That could take decades.

With the achievement of sovereign status, the African states have assumed the burden of coping with poverty, ignorance and disease, and with the demoralizing lack of economic opportunity. Soon after independence, Kenyatta said publicly that there was no option but to look forward:

"Triumph in a struggle of this kind cannot be achieved without a long history of setbacks and sufferings, of failure and humiliation," he said. "But all this is worthwhile, and all can be forgotten, when its outcome is the foundation on which a future can be built. It is the future, my friends, that is living, and the past that is dead."

# FOR FURTHER READING

ATTWOOD, WILLIAM. *The Reds and the Blacks*. New York: Harper & Row, Publishers, 1967.

COLE, SONIA. *The Prehistory of East Africa*. New York: The Macmillan Company, 1963; paperback, New York: New American Library, 1964.

COUPLAND, REGINALD. *East Africa and Its Invaders from the Earliest Times to the Death of Seyyid Said in 1856*. New York: Russell and Russell, 1938; reprinted 1965.

DINESEN, ISAK. *Out of Africa*. New York: Random House, Inc., 1970.

GHAI, DHARAM P. *Portrait of a Minority: Asians in East Africa*. New York: Oxford University Press, 1966.

HARRIES, LYNDON. *Swahili Poetry*. New York: Oxford University Press, 1962.

HILLABY, JOHN D. *Journey to the Jade Sea*. New York: Simon & Schuster, Inc., 1965.

HOBLEY, CHARLES W. *Bantu Beliefs and Magic*. New York: Barnes & Noble, Inc., 1938.

HUGHES, A. J. *East Africa: The Search for Unity*. Baltimore: Penguin Books, Inc., 1963.

HUXLEY, ELSPETH. *The Flame Trees of Thika: Memories of an African Childhood*. New York: William Morrow & Co., Inc., 1959; paperback, New York: Apollo Editions, Inc., 1959.

HUXLEY, ELSPETH. *White Man's Country (Lord Delamere and the Making of Kenya).* 2 volumes, London: Chatto & Windus, 1956.

JACKSON, FREDERICK. *Early Days in East Africa* (British Colonial History Series). New York: Humanities Press, Inc., 1970.

KENYATTA, JOMO. *Facing Mount Kenya.* Elmsford, New York: British Book Centre, Inc., 1956; paperback, New York: Random House, Inc., Vintage Books, 1962.

KIRBY, C. P. *East Africa* (Countries of Today Series). New York: David White Company, 1968.

MARSH, ZOE A. *East Africa Through Contemporary Records.* New York: Cambridge University Press, 1961.

——, and G. W. KINGSNORTH. *An Introduction to the History of East Africa.* (3rd Edition) New York: Cambridge University Press, 1965.

MOOREHEAD, ALAN. *The White Nile.* New York: Harper & Row, Publishers, 1961.

MURDOCK, G. P. *Africa: Its Peoples and Their Cultural History.* New York: McGraw-Hill Book Company, 1959.

WELBOURN, F. B. *Religion and Politics in Uganda 1952–1962.* Pub. by East African Publishing House, Evanston, Illinois: Northwestern University Press, 1965.

# INDEX

Picture Credits: Lawrence Fellows, i, v, 20, 52, 109, 129; Historical Pictures Service—Chicago, 32, 38, 41, 45; Kenya Information Services, 13, 18, 59, 78–79, 124–125; Monkmeyer Press Photo Service, vi (Philcarol), 24, 61, 93, 118; Nancy Palmer Photo Agency, 100 (Mohamed Amin); Pictorial Parade, Inc., 64 (A.F.P.), 99 (London Daily Express); Radio Times Hulton Picture Library, 68, 88; Rapho Guillumette, title page (Lynn Millar McLaren), 106 (Marc & Evelyne Bernheim); United Nations, 6, 10–11, 70, 116, 122, 127, 131; United Press International Photo, 73, 83, 91, 113. Cover photo by Giorgio Ricatto—FPG.